Contents

The Theory into Practice Series

This exciting new series fills a significant gap in the market for short, user-friendly texts, written by experts, that succinctly introduce sets of theoretical ideas, relate them clearly to practice issues, and guide the reader to further learning. They particularly address discrimination, oppression, equality and diversity. They can be read either as general overviews of particular areas of theory and practice, or as foundations for further study. The series will be invaluable across the human services, including social work and social care; youth and community work; criminal and community justice work; counselling; advice work; housing; and aspects of health care.

About the Series Editor

Neil Thompson is a Director of Avenue Consulting Ltd (*www.avenueconsulting. co.uk*), a company offering training and consultancy in relation to social work and human relations issues. He was formerly Professor of Applied Social Studies at Staffordshire University. He has over 100 publications to his name, including best-selling textbooks, papers in scholarly journals and training and open learning materials.

Neil is a Fellow of the Chartered Institute of Personnel and Development, the Institute of Training and Occupational Learning and the Royal Society of Arts (elected on the basis of his contribution to organisational learning). He is the editor of the *British Journal of Occupational Learning* (*wwwtraininginstitute.co.uk*). He was also responsible for the setting up of the self-help website, *www.human solutions.org.uk*. His personal website is at www.neilthompson.info.

Prospective authors wishing to make a contribution to the *Theory into Practice* series should contact Neil via his company website, www.avenueconsulting. co.uk.

Series Editor's Foreword

About the series

The relationship between theory and practice is one that has puzzled practitioners and theorists alike for some considerable time, and there still remains considerable debate about how the two interconnect. However, what is clear is that it is dangerous to tackle the complex problems encountered in 'people work' without having at least a basic understanding of what makes people tick, of how the social context plays a part in both the problems we address and the solutions we seek. Working with people and their problems is difficult and demanding work. To try to undertake it without being armed with a sound professional knowledge base is a very risky strategy indeed, and potentially a disastrous one.

An approach to practice based mainly on guesswork, untested assumptions, habit and copying others is clearly not one that can be supported. Good practice must be an *informed* practice, with actions based, as far as possible, on reasoning, understanding and evidence. This series is intended to develop just such good practice by providing:

- an introductory overview of a particular area of theory or professional knowledge;
- an exploration of how it relates to practice issues;
- a consideration of how the theory base can help tackle discrimination and oppression; and
- a guide to further learning.

The texts in the series are written by people with extensive knowledge and practical experience in the fields concerned and are intended as an introduction to the wider and more in-depth literature base.

About this book

This particular text, with its focus on religion and spirituality, makes an invaluable contribution to our understanding of the challenges involved in the human services. Bernard Moss points out that this subject matter has tended to be neglected in professional education and is only now beginning to be taken seriously. Religion can be a very controversial and emotive subject, provoking strong reactions both for and against. In this carefully crafted text, the author succeeds in presenting the key issues in an accessible and balanced way, enabling readers to make their own minds up and draw their own conclusions, rather than feel pressured in a particular direction.

Spirituality, too, is a contentious subject that can, in some quarters at least, generate more heat than light, but once again, Bernard Moss's sensitive and skilful treatment of the issues succeeds in presenting a very helpful exposition and analysis of the 'meaning making' that underpins spirituality.

This is an outstanding piece of work and deserves to become a classic in the field.

Neil Thompson, Series Editor

To Sheila
Who has enriched my own journey and pilgrimage
more than she will ever realise.

About the author

Bernard Moss is a Principal Lecturer in Social Work and Applied Social Studies and a Learning and Teaching Fellow at Staffordshire University. In 2004 he became a National Teaching Fellow of the Higher Education Academy. His teaching interests include mediation; death, dying and bereavement; divorce and separation, and spirituality in health and social care. He is the co-ordinator of the Centre for Health and Spirituality in the Faculty of Health and Sciences at Staffordshire University. His previous experience includes university chaplaincy and being a leader of a faith community. He has been a marriage counsellor, probation officer and a family mediator. His publications include a chapter on Spirituality in Thompson (2002a) *Loss and Grief: A Guide for Human Services Practitioners*, Basingstoke, Palgrave, and a training pack on Issues of Grief and Loss. His research interests include evaluating the contribution which faith communities can make to enhancing social capital in their localities.

Acknowledgements

It is impossible fully to acknowledge the debt of gratitude which I owe to so many people who will have contributed to this book, often without knowing it, in both large ways and small. Anyone who seeks to deal with the great themes of religion and spirituality will have drunk deep from a variety of wells, and I am no exception. The moments of insight which point us to 'the beyondness of things' remind us that it is possible to see everyday life as part of a journey, or at times a pilgrimage even, where issues of meaning and purpose become important signposts. To everyone therefore who has shared my own journey, and helped me catch some glimpses of 'otherness' along the way, I am enormously grateful.

   The book itself would not have been possible without the encouragement, colleagueship and friendship of Professor Neil Thompson who has helped me begin to see clearly how important these issues are for social work practice and in the wider context of a variety of human services. Professor Leola Furman has been grappling with these issues alongside Ed Canda and others in the USA and Canada for nearly 30 years, and is leading the field with some distinguished academic writing. Her inspiration, insight and friendship have served as an 'illumination to my own path' as I have tried to explore these issues in a UK context. Professor Mike Dent and John Pierson, my PhD supervisors at Staffordshire University, have shared a particular journey with me as I have grappled with the themes of spirituality and social work education and practice, and in supportive and encouraging ways have opened up more and more issues for me to explore. Professor Peter Gilbert has helped me to understand the relevance of these issues to the wide field of mental health, and not least to the key theme of recovery. My particular thanks go to Jenny Nemko and Sidney Morris for enriching my understanding of Jewish perspectives, and to Rana Tufail for his wisdom in helping me appreciate and understand something more about Islam. Mike Wolfe, Stoke on Trent's first elected Mayor, has influenced my thinking about how to celebrate diversity more than he will ever know. I am also grateful to Santokh Gill, from Staffordshire University, for his diligence in pulling together statistical information and key references from relevant legislation. None of these colleagues, however, can be held accountable for any of this book's inadequacies.

If however this book serves as a modest signpost to help others explore the fascinating and important interface between religion, spirituality and the rich variety of human services, I shall be content.

Introduction

Prologue: a personal perspective

It has been drilled into students in a number of disciplines for many years now that 'self-location' is an essential ingredient in their reflective practice. It makes a big difference whether you write from a male or female perspective; or from a black, Asian or white point of view; whether your sexuality is gay or straight, and whether you write from a disabled or non-disabled perspective. The central issue is that who we are and where we come from fundamentally affect our values, assumptions and perspectives. We owe it to others to make this as clear as we can, to help them in their own explorations, rather than assume that we have achieved an Olympian detachment in communicating eternal truth. There may be some, of course, who feel that it is possible, and desirable, that such issues are taught in an objective, dispassionate way, and who feel that the value base of the teacher or author can be sufficiently muted in order to achieve objectivity. I have to say, however, that I cannot agree with this position.

I feel therefore that it is important for you, as you read this book, to know a little of where I am coming from, so that you can interpret what I have to say accordingly. Being white, I cannot hope to do full justice to a black perspective – and with black identity and culture sometimes being associated with faith communities, this is something I am bound not to get fully right. Being male, I cannot hope to do full justice to a female perspective – and with so much oppression against women stemming from religious organisations, I am bound not to get this fully right either. Being heterosexual, I cannot hope to do full justice to a gay perspective – and with so much anti-gay oppression stemming from religious organisations, I am bound not to get this fully right. Being a social work academic, with practice experience in probation, counselling and mediation, I cannot hope to do full justice to those other human services professionals who will have an interest in these issues, although strenuous efforts have been made to ensure that this book has as wide an appeal as possible. Being Christian, I cannot hope to do full justice either to those who belong to other faith communities, or to those who feel more at home with the label of humanist, atheist or agnostic – and with so much Christian imperialism to cope with, I can understand if everything I say is treated, by some at least, with more than healthy skepticism.

But all of us have to be true to ourselves and to speak the truth as we perceive it. From where I am coming from (in contrast to the perspectives which I cannot fully own, as indicated above), the issues of religion and spirituality take us to the very heart of what it means to be human and to be living together in society. For me there are profound connections between religion, spirituality and social justice; between the 'tap root' of compassion and the human rights of those who are marginalised, oppressed and victimised. They are of deep significance, in my opinion, and deserve to be taken seriously by anyone who works professionally in the human services.

Not that this is necessarily one-way traffic. In matters to do with religion and spirituality, there has been a perceived hostility towards some Christian and Muslim students, who have felt that their faith commitment was being devalued by both academic staff and other students on their professional courses (Channer, 1998). Many curricula, for example, have often dealt with these issues through neglect, much to the consternation of students who come from faith communities and who wish to explore the relationship between their faith-based values and their professional values. There is certainly a feeling in some disciplines, that to raise issues of religion and spirituality is to go against the tide of contemporary professional education for human service workers. But the tide is beginning to turn.

I have a passionate interest in these vital topics. I believe that, at their best, they are liberating and life enhancing, and should take their rightful place within the practice curriculum, and be taken seriously by everyone involved as part of best practice. That same commitment to best practice, however, will also be active in recognising and challenging areas where religion and spirituality have become oppressive in the lives of people with whom human service workers are professionally engaged.

In this book I have suggested that spirituality may be understood as *what we do to give expression to our chosen world-view*. I hope that this definition will prove 'fit for purpose' as we explore these crucial issues and seek to relate them to our professional practice.

> We shall not cease from exploration,
> And the end of all our exploring
> Will be to arrive where we started
> And know the place for the first time.
>
> T.S. Eliot Four Quartets. Little Gidding. V lines 239–242

Setting the scene

'If I were you I wouldn't start from here!'

This jocular riposte, occasionally offered to the bewildered traveller struggling to reach a destination without reliable signposts, captures something of the dilemma about how to begin a book about religion and spirituality. For some, the very title may be off-putting: this is territory which feels distinctly uncomfortable and unfamiliar, and even to ask for directions causes them some consternation or unease. For others, there may be a contrasting sense of excitement *precisely because* this is familiar territory, and they feel very much at home here, and secretly wish that many more would join them.

Already we see that the danger of polarisation has been raised in the opening paragraph, with some people feeling that this is definitely not for them, while others warmly welcome the enterprise. This should come as no surprise, for these are topics which are notorious for setting people's teeth on edge, and not just at parties. In the professional training courses designed to prepare people for a career as human services practitioners, it is as likely as not that the issues of religion and spirituality will either receive scant attention, or be relegated to the domain of personal interests or hobbies, like rock climbing or choral singing. If that is your scene, then go for it if you must, but don't bring it into your professional life. There are other professionals whose job it is to deal with those issues: they have no place in the contemporary human services practitioner's tool kit.

Part of the difficulty, therefore, in starting such a discussion is precisely this pre-existing polarisation which seems to be set on predetermined train lines of thought – occasionally there may be some parallel journeys where people can call across to each other, but more often than not the train lines go off in different directions, or achieve the buffeting and disconcerting effect as two trains hurtle past each other in opposite directions. No wonder these subjects tend to be avoided. As we observed at the outset, if I were you I wouldn't start from here.

But times, they are a-changing. Within the nursing sphere, the spiritual and religious needs of patients have long been recognised, with increasingly multi-faith chaplaincies being established. In the sphere of social work education the need for social workers to take issues of religion and spirituality seriously has begun to be recognised. The former Central Council for Education and Training in Social Work (CCETSW), for example, published a monograph entitled 'Visions of Reality: religion and ethnicity in social work' in which Patel, Naik and Humphries (1997) argue that:

> everyone is influenced by religion and religious practices whether they are believers, agnostics or atheists. Social service users are no exception. Yet religious cultural practices, group and individual spirituality, religious divisions and religion as therapy have had no place in social work education and practice, even though social work has its origins in religious philanthropy. Ever the invisible presence in modern social work, its place should be recognised and taken account of in the work of the profession. (p. ii)

The implication of this 'invisible presence' for other professionals is clear. Whatever the particular emphasis of the work – be it youth or community work; criminal or community justice; counselling; advice work; social work, nursing or health care; policing or prison-based work – there will be occasions when issues of religion and spirituality need not only to be recognised, but also taken seriously in the multicultural, multi-faith societies of England, Scotland, Wales, Northern Ireland, and beyond.

This book offers an introduction, therefore, to a wide range of human services practitioners who recognise the importance of taking these issues seriously, whatever their own personal 'take' on them may be. Its starting point is a celebration of diversity, and the need to treat others with dignity and respect, especially when views and opinions differ widely. This is not the place, however, for a debate about the relative merits of the claims to 'ultimate truth' made by some religions. Readers who wish to explore the apologetics for a particular religion will need to undertake this as a distinctly separate enterprise. Neverthe-less, an important dimension of the book will be a discussion about the extent to which religion and spirituality are perceived as having an 'emancipatory/liberating/life-enhancing effect' or a 'negative/oppressive/life-denying' impact upon people's lives, and this will inevitably involve a range of value judgments on the part of both the author and the reader. Whether we like it or not, we will find that we are being drawn into subjective evaluations as professional workers when we start taking these issues seriously for ourselves and for those with whom we work.

The book has four main parts. In Part One the theory base is explored, in the course of which there is a discussion about the concepts of religion and spirituality, and some definitions offered. This also includes an overview of some of the key legislation which urges human services practitioners to take these issues seriously. Part Two begins to explore some key practice issues, which lead into Part Three where the focus is upon anti-discriminatory and anti-oppressive practice issues. Part Four offers some suggestions for further learning, reading and study.

It is worth adding a brief note about two phrases which will be used regularly throughout this book. 'Human services practitioners' is a phrase which has become more widely used in recent years to include the whole range of professional people who work in a formal caring capacity. These include social workers, probation officers, youth workers; advice workers; counsellors; criminal and community justice workers; and all who work in a health care capacity. Although not the most elegant of phrases, it is intended to be a comprehensive and inclusive term which captures the essence of the work across many disciplines. We are dealing with *human* services which are dealing with human problems and concerns all the time. This book has been written with this in mind, and argues that issues of religion and spirituality also operate in the same area. We hope too that it will be of interest to people who work specifically in faith-based organisations.

Faith-based organisations (FBOs) is another phrase which seeks to be comprehensive and inclusive in its scope. Admittedly less elegant than its synonym 'faith communities', it is nevertheless a useful compendium designed to include the wide variety of religious groupings and meeting places for worship and community outreach. In that sense it has a wider scope than faith communities because it will include community-based initiatives which may be separate from the worship-based activities of, for example, churches or mosques.

We turn now to the important topic of the theoretical underpinnings for these issues which will be discussed in Part One.

Part One: The Theory Base

Chapter 1
Religion and Spirituality: Towards Some Definitions

The development of a theory base upon which to build sound anti-discriminatory practice across a range of social care professions is not as straightforward in this area as it would be for developing appropriate intervention strategies for working with older people, or in youth work, or in nursing practice. As we have already suggested, the concepts of religion and spirituality can be so varied in interpretation that it is difficult to achieve an agreed common ground.

This is not to deny the usefulness of various academic disciplines in helping us to understand the phenomenon of religion and spirituality. The sociology of religion, for example, has made a powerful contribution to our understanding of these topics. Studies in lifespan development have also helped us to understand the complex web of our deep-seated human 'drives' and needs, as well as understanding some of the psychological aspects of religious experience. Any major reputable textbook from either of these disciplines will introduce the reader to the main themes and developments in this area. It is not within the purpose of this book, however, to offer a detailed discussion of the main features of this complex academic terrain, although a brief synopsis will be offered to help set the scene.

Two main aspects of a theory base however are fundamental. First, a discussion of the main themes of religion and spirituality is essential, but in a way which has a direct bearing and relevance for the professional disciplines being addressed in this book. This inevitably will focus on the issues of definition, and what are the 'touching places' which human services professionals can identify from their own practice.

Secondly, it will be important to review the 'legislative imperative' which has placed the issues of religion and spirituality so firmly onto the human services agenda. Best practice must now take these issues into account and deal with them seriously. They cannot be left to the individual whim or discretion of the worker, trainer or teacher, as to whether they are tackled or not. The various strands of this 'legislative imperative' therefore may justifiably be regarded as an important part of the theory base for these topics.

Before we go any further, therefore, it is important to attempt some definition of the terms being used in this book, principally those of 'religion' and 'spirituality'. These are issues which have fascinated sociologists and theologians alike, and it will come as no surprise to a reader new to this territory that the further one gets into this issue of definitions the more complex the debate becomes. Inevitably, the definitions which will be offered for this book will be hotly contested by sociological and theological specialists, but without some understanding of the terms being used, there is a danger that they can mean different things to different people (see Moss, 2002, pp. 34ff).

This is a debate which is familiar to several professional groups, including nursing. Tanyi (2002), noting that spiritual care has been part of nursing history since ancient times, comments that:

> In the last few decades there has been a resurgence of spiritual discourse, as scientific-based approaches are not fully able to address many fundamental human problems such as persistent pain. Furthermore, people are searching for peace, meaningful lives. (p. 501)

At one level, of course, the question of definition, at least as far as religion is concerned, seems to be easily answered. By 'religion' is meant those major groupings within global societies which have particular names and identifiable sets of beliefs – for example, Islam, Christianity, Judaism, Buddhism and many more. In their study of attitudes towards religion and spirituality, Canda and Furman (1999, p. 54) used the following operational definition: 'Religion was defined as "an organized structured set of beliefs and practices shared by a community related to spirituality"'.

Within these religious systems, there is a belief in the supernatural – a divine being or beings or spiritual forces which to some extent influence the behaviour of human beings. According to Robertson (1970, p. 47) religion: 'refers to the existence of supernatural beings that have a governing effect on life'.

It is important to recognise that the word 'religion' is often applied with equal ease to a much wider range of activities than the so-called mainstream religions. These include many New Religious Movements (NRMs). Hunt (2002) notes that there are now nearly 2,600 new religions, and comments that:

> contemporary NRMs . . . range from those such as the Unification Church, the Children of God, the Divine Light Mission, Krishna Consciousness, Scientology, Rastafarianism, Transcendental Meditation and the Rajneeshes. Many of these appear to have little in common. (pp. 146–147)

For a discussion on the situation in the United States of America, see Canda and Furman (1999, pp. 84 ff).

If, however, we add the observation that cult followings of sporting and contemporary music stars, not to mention the avid support of many football and other sporting teams, are also often described as being 'religions', then we see very acutely how important the problem of definition has become. As Hunt (2002) comments:

> Religion is what individuals and societies say it is. If a soccer fan regarded the support of his [*sic*] team as a form of 'religion' who could legitimately question the claim?

We begin to understand even more how utter bewilderment can set in for people who try to understand these issues and to explore what each of these various religious groups believes, but then give up the quest as 'mission impossible' – or just as likely, 'mission irrelevant'.

A way forward?

One way through this increasingly complex maze is to approach the issue from another direction, so that instead of asking ourselves what this or that particular religion stands for, or what its main tenets of faith are, we ask ourselves what a religion achieves for those who subscribe to it. This follows a tradition which the sociologist Emile Durkheim developed, in which he argued that one of the main functions of religion is to promote the well-being, stability, and integration and social cohesion of society (Hunt, 2002, p. 8) – in other words, focus attention on: what contribution does religion make to society; what *function* does it fulfil for those who subscribe to it, and for the society in which it is set?

A functionalist perspective on religion clearly has limitations. It does not do justice, for example, to the sense of awe and mystery and 'otherness' – theologians use the word 'transcendence' to point to this – which is at the heart certainly of the major monotheistic religions. Nor does it particularly help in the quest for testing the truth claims of particular religious groupings, or in grappling with the skepticism which grew out of the Enlightenment and which predicted the demise of religion in the advance of scientific rationalism. All of these issues are of great interest to sociologists of religion and theologians, but lie outside the immediate scope of this book. Another criticism, however, which will be central to our discussion is that it does not do justice to the ways in which, within some religions at least, there is a strong prophetic and critical challenge to the social order of the day. This is a theme to which we shall strongly return.

Human services practitioners, however, are likely to find the questions and issues which arise out of a functionalist perspective particularly useful, whether or not they themselves belong to a faith-based organisation (FBO). It means that they can leave to one side, for the most part, the details of belief and doctrine to which a particular religious group happens to subscribe, and ask instead questions such as:

- What does it mean for this person to belong to this FBO?
- What needs does it fulfil?

- What sense of meaning and purpose does it give to those who belong to it?
- What is the world-view to which they now subscribe?
- What actions and activities flow from belonging to this group?

These are all crucial questions, and illustrate what Patel *et al*. (1998) meant when they observed that if you 'touch religion, you touch a person's deepest being' (p. ii). This is not to say that this will be true for everyone who has a religious dimension in their lives. Far from it – for some people religious observances are no more than social rituals. What Patel is referring to is when people take their religion with the utmost seriousness and allow it to shape their understanding of the world and their place within it. This is what Mannheim (1936) meant when he said:

> We belong to a group not because we are born into it, not merely because we profess to belong to it, nor finally because we give it our loyalty and allegiance, *but primarily because we see the world and certain things in the world the way it does*. (pp. 21–22, emphasis added)

And it is here, perhaps, that we find one of the major 'touching places' for much of the work which human services practitioners undertake. Whether it be in a counselling relationship where deep-seated issues of meaning and relationships are being explored; or in social work with its engagement with people in stressful, challenging, and at times abusive relationships; or in criminal justice work where people's behaviour raises deep issues of what drives them and gives them a 'buzz'; or in advice work where often people are overwhelmed by despair as a result of the escalating burden of debt and of trying to cope when the odds are stacked against them; or in youth work where young people are often trying to deal with the powerful tensions between their surging potential and limited opportunities; or in nursing where issues of health and illness, well-being and recovery, sickness and death are part of the daily round: in all these areas of work, the questions which have been suggested from a functionalist perspective on religion all have relevance.

Or do they? For there is an immediate caveat here. If it is being suggested in all the areas of work outlined above that people who use these services all come from a religious background, then this would clearly need to be challenged, certainly in the UK context. The chances are that the vast majority of them would deny having any religious background or allegiance at all. But the questions still have relevance, which is why for many people the context for this whole debate needs to be widened considerably by bringing into the discussion the concept of spirituality.

Here we begin to see why we struggled to make a start with this discussion, and suggested that 'if I were you I wouldn't start from here'. For if religious concepts and 'holy-talk' are increasingly being seen as the territory of the 'holy few', then spirituality, perhaps, fares no better in a secular society. Spirituality is admittedly difficult to define, but Swinton (2001) argues that:

> whilst people may be becoming less *religious*, it would be a mistake to assume from that that they are necessarily become less spiritual, or that they are no longer searching for a sense of transcendence and spiritual fulfillment . . . spiritual beliefs and desires that were once located primarily within institutionalised religions have migrated across to other forms of spirituality . . . spirituality has broadened in meaning into a more diffuse human need what can be met quite apart from institutionalised religious structures. (pp. 11–12)

A lot of work has been done in this field already, not least in the United States of America, where for the past few decades academics and practitioners alike have been wrestling with these issues. Canda and Furman (1999), for example, argue that, far from being an optional 'add-on', spirituality fulfils a unifying holistic function for every human being, whether or not they subscribe to a religious framework of belief. They argue that those who:

> study religion and spirituality assume that there is an aspect of the person that strives for a sense of meaning, purpose and morality (Eliade, 1959; James, 1982; Lesser and Vogt, 1972). This 'spiritual' aspect motivates experience and action to engage self with the world . . . it orients the person and groups towards ultimacy, that is, things that are given ultimate value and priority . . . It is our position that this spiritual aspect is fundamental to human nature and infuses other aspects. Indeed, the spiritual aspect impels us to give meaning and purpose to our bodies and biological functions, our thoughts and feelings, and our relationships with other people, and the rest of the universe. (p. 47)

This argument led them to offer this definition of spirituality:

> The search for meaning, purpose and morally fulfilling relation with self, other people, the encompassing universe, and ultimate reality, however a person understands it . . . it was explained that spirituality can be 'expressed through religious forms but is not limited to them'. (p. 9)

Maybe for some, this language feels a bit 'high-falutin', especially if relating to the 'encompassing universe and ultimate reality' appears to be one challenge too far. It may seem to some rather like the child's early self-addressed envelope which begins with a specific house, road, town and country and then moves through the continent, the world, the universe and to infinity! That all may be true, but the address works perfectly well without those wider contexts being added. The big question for our discussion, therefore, is whether these wider contexts of religion and spirituality need to be included in our professional practice, or whether we, and those who come to us, can get by perfectly well without them.

It may be helpful, therefore, to lay alongside all of this two other comments which may help us engage with these issues, and to understand more clearly what Canda and Furman are seeking to articulate.

Lloyd (1996) notes, in her work with parents who are struggling to cope with the death of a child, 'the frequency with which professional bodies encounter the 'Why?' question. This is the question which:

> at times of great crisis and loss is thrown directly or indirectly at many people who work in human services, be they doctors, social workers, nurses, care assistants, counsellors, youth workers, leaders of faith communities . . . the big question – the really big question – is far less easy to handle. (Moss, 2002, p. 35)

This 'big question' is the one which at times desperately seeks to find meaning in, and for, events which happen to us. This has led Morgan (1993) to suggest that the search for meaning is ultimately what spirituality is all about, and to argue that: 'Human spirituality is to seek an answer to the question: "how can you make sense out of a world which does not seem to be intrinsically reasonable?" ' (p. 6). Or to put it another way, spirituality asks us what our world-view is, and how we try to make sense of the things which happen to us.

But we need to return to Canda and Furman who also argue that, far from being egocentric:

> this understanding of spirituality not only helps people achieve a sense of wholeness and personal integrity, but also fosters a sense of responsibility for, and connection with others. The self is no longer defined in egocentric ways, but rather in relation to other people. (p. 48)

Two points deserve to be highlighted here. First, these are issues which affect everyone, whether or not they are articulated. Spirituality, in other words, is a sort of 'short-hand' way of asking the fundamental questions about ourselves – what makes us 'tick'; what is important to us; what gives us a sense of meaning and purpose in our lives. In short, it asks of people what is their world-view. These are issues which in a wide variety of ways human services practitioners grapple with in their everyday work, even if the concept of spirituality is never specifically mentioned. This 'wider context', therefore, as mentioned above, is far from being irrelevant to much of the work we undertake.

Second, spirituality has an outward-looking dimension to it. Here is offered a litmus test of genuine spirituality in the extent to which it 'fosters a sense of responsibility for . . . others'. At this point there is considerable overlap between religious and spiritual perspectives, as evidenced by the testimony of people who have chosen, or felt inwardly compelled into, a social caring career, and for whom Canda and Furman's apothegm rings true: 'spirituality is the heart of helping'. Not that human services practitioners should claim a monopoly of this, however – far from it. This is an energy which is part of the potential of every human being. It is just that human services practitioners have the privilege to be instrumental in helping other people both to claim and to release that energy in their own lives, whether that is through counselling; advice work; engaging with young people; healing and nursing; or the many facets of social work practice.

This recognition of energy and potential to care for others has received a new emphasis in recent years as many agencies have begun to recognise the contribution which faith-based organisations can make, and are already making, to the enrichment of their local communities. Again, a lot of work has been undertaken in the States in this area (for example, Cnaan, 1999; Nesbitt, 2001; Wood, 1997), but within the Four Nations some significant work has been taking place to explore and develop the notion of social capital and how faith-based organisations can make serious contributions to this field (Farnell *et al.*, 2003; Harris *et al.*, 2003). These developments locate spirituality within a framework of social justice and reintroduce the point made earlier in this introduction about the prophetic strand in some religious traditions which challenges the ways in which society is structured, and which demands a more just and equitable social order.

This takes us into a broader definition of spirituality which can include religious perspectives within it, and certainly encompasses the search for meaning and purpose, but then goes on to ask the functionalist questions: What difference does all of this make to you and to what you do with your life? What impact does it have upon how you treat other people both individually and within communities?

It is at this point that we may attempt a definition of spirituality which can be useful for human services practitioners who wish to explore some of these central issues: *Spirituality may be defined for our purposes as what we do to give expression to our chosen world-view.*

This world-view may be specifically religious – we may belong to a Christian, Jewish, Muslim, Hindu or one of many other faith-based communities, which give us a sense of community and purpose, and an outlook upon the world which shapes our thinking and our social action. It also encourages us to undertake certain activities such as shared worship and prayer.

This world-view may most definitely not be religious – we may feel more comfortable with being agnostic or atheist or humanist – we may define our position as being existentialist – this too will shape our outlook upon the world and our social action, and what we choose to do and not to do to express our convictions.

This world-view may be shared by others in very specific ways, in that we choose to belong to a group which shares and explores and develops the implications for social action; or we may hold it in isolation in a more individualistic way. In the end, the issues will be similar for us and for those with whom we seek to work.

What we cannot do is to ignore these issues or pretend that they are peripheral to our practice. Whether the practice and behaviours which spring from people's particular world-views are liberating or oppressive is of course an issue of fundamental importance for practice, and will receive substantial treatment later on in this book.

Having reached this point in the discussion, one crucial insight should have been achieved. What we have been discussing is not a topic which is restricted to service user territory, from which the professional worker can somehow feel detached. The definition of spirituality being offered in this book does not allow such tidy, sanitised boundaries to be drawn. Instead, it draws us all in, and encourages us to peer behind the labels we place upon each other, and to acknowledge that this is an enterprise in which we are all involved by virtue of our nature as human beings. We all struggle to make sense of what happens to us, and who is to say that one person's struggle is of greater or less value than another's? We owe each other the dignity and respect of recognising that we are all on a similar journey of discovery.

This has a clear resonance with the tenets of best practice across various caring professions. The core values of dignity and respect; of recognising the intrinsic value and worth of each individual (whether or not we subscribe to a religious perspective which holds that ultimate value is derived from a supreme Being); of recognising that loving, sacrificial caring for others is a potential within all people – these form the value base of how human services practitioners aspire to regard those who come to them for help, and how they themselves would wish to be regarded in return.

It also is a challenge to everyone working in the human services to take a measure of responsibility for their own well-being in this regard. Practitioners are involved with people often at crisis points in their lives, where the big questions of meaning and purpose are raised, explicitly or implicitly. If they themselves as workers are not comfortable in this area, then they are not likely to feel able to be open and helpful to the people who need to feel listened to and valued at the very point where they need it most. But it is precisely at this point that some workers are tempted to take flight.

> They may well struggle with the 'Why?' question when it is asked, and each of them may feel it is best left to someone else to tackle – 'someone who knows about these things'. The assumption is that spirituality, however it is defined, is outwith the professional expertise or even concern of most human services practitioners. As Lloyd (1997) so aptly observes 'a spiritual dimension is not generally seen as part of the liberal-thinking, politically-aware social worker's anti-discriminatory took kit'. (Moss, 2002, p. 183)

The argument of this book seeks to turn this observation on its head, and to assert that any human services practitioner – be they social worker; counsellor; advice worker; youth worker; criminal or community justice worker; nurse – who fails to take the spiritual dimension of people's lives into account, or who fails to take it into account for their own lives, is not meeting the demands of best practice, and is not likely to be able to offer anything like the holistic service to which people are entitled.

A further implication of this understanding of spirituality needs to be included in this theoretical perspective. It might be thought from the argument developed so far that it is a case of 'anything goes', and that there are no moral or professional benchmarks to guide human behaviour or professional intervention. 'If my spirituality says it is OK to treat others in a particular way, who are you to deny me that right?'

In some ways this goes to the heart of some of the dilemmas that arise from practice situations, but it also raises the issue which has been touched on already, namely the extent to which religion and spirituality are life-enhancing or life-diminishing activities. It also raises the issue, which perhaps is starkest in the three main monotheistic religions – Judaism, Christianity and Islam – about the extent to which the gendered and heterosexist nature of religious language and authority has been responsible for the systematic devaluing of women, and the refusal to acknowledge any validity for same-sex relationships.

Some of these issues are of such importance that it is necessary to consider them in the context of the theoretical base being explored in this chapter. Of necessity the focus for this part of the discussion needs to be narrowed down to the three main monotheistic religions, for the following reasons. First, to attempt to cover every aspect of religion would prove too time- and space-consuming for the scope of this book. Second, the issues can be most clearly identified and discussed by limiting the focus in this way. And third, for many people these issues are most appropriately laid at the door of these three religious systems. Finally, any principles established from this discussion can then be considered to see if they can be applied to any other religion.

Interestingly, the issues which need to be raised can all be understood from a similar functionalist perspective as has already been outlined above. The 'case against' these religions, if we may state it thus, often has less to do with the truth claims which each makes, or the details of the doctrinal dogmas which each espouses, and far more to do with how the adherents of these religions have behaved towards others. It is precisely the apparent *function* of these religions to cause some of their followers to act in oppressive ways towards others which has led not only to suspicion, but to a 'root and branch' rejection of them by many people. It is perfectly possible, therefore, to understand how a human services worker who has adopted this stance on moral or ethical grounds would find it difficult to agree with the definition of best practice outlined above, where a sensitivity to spirituality is being recommended.

It is at this point, however, that the world-view perspective comes into play again. Supporters of religion and their antagonists (if we may speak so crudely for a moment) both have to find a way of coming to terms with the positive and negative aspects of religion, without simplistically and uncritically accepting or rejecting the 'whole package'. Looking at this theologically, there needs to be an understanding of good and evil within their world-view, where full justice is done to both. As Patel *et al.* (1998) so aptly put it:

Human beings are able to commit unbelievable atrocities in the name of religion, and to rise to heights of courage and sacrifice for their faith. Any profession which aims to understand the underlying motivation of people should not ignore the place of religion in their lives. (p. 9)

Again, it is not the intention of this book to rehearse all the arguments for and against the existence of a divine Being, or to explore the complex doctrinal subtleties within these three religions about the nature of good and evil. It will be helpful, however, as part of the theoretical underpinning, to examine at least some of the main issues which impinge upon human services practice, and to understand why some people remain firmly convinced that religion and spirituality should have no place within their professional remit.

Chapter 2
Religion: The Case Against

Although the concept of spirituality has become increasingly popular and important, it is helpful for a moment to lay it to one side and focus on the ways in which religion has been challenged from a range of theoretical perspectives. Some of these critiques will be applicable also to spirituality, but not necessarily all of them. It is easier for us to concentrate on religion therefore in this section of the discussion.

Some theoretical perspectives

Without doubt the seminal influence of Marx and Freud upon the issue of religion has left a legacy of mistrust many decades after the first impact of their writings. Stated bluntly, Marx chastised the religion of his day (principally Christianity) for diverting the attention of people away from the harsh political challenges of the day by offering them (in the now famous cliché) 'pie in the sky when you die'. Religion was seen as a preparation for a better life after death, and for Marx this apparent denial of the importance of social justice here and now was totally unacceptable. Whether or not we accept the Marxist critique of power in society, the challenge to religion was sharp and powerful. He has left a persuasive legacy which those who belong to faith-based organisations have had to take seriously, not least in their contemporary theology and practice of social justice issues.

Freud approached the topic from a different perspective of course, with his deep fascination with how human beings 'tick'. His investigations into what he called the 'id', the 'ego' and the 'superego' convinced him that there are profound drives deep within human beings which we need to understand in order to live satisfying lives. The capacity of human beings to project deep-seated needs, longings and aspirations upon others, or beyond others, led him to suggest that (again to put it bluntly) religion was an infantile misplaced projection of various deep-seated needs upon a mythical deity who only existed as a result of these projections. If people could only deal with these needs appropriately, then they would see that religion is an ultimate fantasy, and no more.

Although the work of these two seminal figures has been extensively critiqued, and their respective disciplines have made great strides forward in their understanding and analyses, it is likely that the profound skepticism about religion shared by many people has been fuelled to a considerable extent by the analyses of Marx and Freud, even if their original work understandably now feels dated.

The third major player in this field has been the development of secularisation, to which without doubt Marx and Freud made an early contribution, but which can also be seen to be the natural outcome of the Enlightenment, and the move towards scientific rationalism. Hunt (2002) sums this up in his comment that:

> Stemming from the Enlightenment, the hope for a secular society began as an academic response to the dominance of the Christian Church and continued as a reaction to religious authority by those who are inclined towards atheism. In good tradition, many sociologists have since viewed religious belief as an intellectual error which the progress of science and rationality would ultimately weaken to the point of disappearance. (p. 15)

It is worth identifying some of the themes which contribute to this general critique, not least because they still enjoy some popularity. Although religion has often been seen as a 'haven' where people can escape from, or at least have a breather from the harsh realities of life (Marx referred to religion once as the 'heart of a heartless world') – a serious criticism has been the disempowering nature of religion. Feuerbach (1941), for example, believed that human beings projected the ideals and values which they produced as part of their cultural development onto divine beings, which tended to produce a sense of alienation. What hope did human beings have of emulating these divine values? So long as human beings regarded themselves as essentially flawed and helpless, the chances of improving society were very limited. It also lent itself to the 'deferred gratification' criticism of religion, associated with Marx's famous phrase 'opium of the people'. All would be well when you died and went to heaven; but as far as challenging and changing an unjust world was concerned, religion was no earthly use whatsoever.

Ironically, for Feuerbach, it was precisely this realisation which could release positive energy in people. Once they recognised the capacity in human beings for being loving and creative, they could escape from this alienation and begin to work for a better world. This too reflects Marx's view that the principal human concern had to be with the material improvement of an unjust society for the benefit of all its members. The heavenly rewards of a religion which seemed unconcerned with social justice was simply an irrelevance, and a dangerous one at that.

In apparent contrast, Durkheim (1912) argued for the importance of religion as a cohesive influence upon a community, and stressed the significance of the 'sacred' as separate from the 'profane' or everyday life. Society needs the 'sacred' to be reminded of its core social values, and to provide a mechanism through its various rituals for social cohesion. Much of Durkheim's work was drawn from his studies of Australian aboriginal societies which provided evidence, in his view, for the essential – or elementary – nature and role of religion. Where he seems to draw much closer to Feuerbach and Marx, however, is in his analysis of the way in which modern society was developing. He believed that traditional religion was fast disappearing – 'the old gods are dead' is how he expressed it. He seemed to suggest, however, that the development of secular forms of social cohesion and common political values would take over from traditional religion and perform a similar, equally important function.

With these seminal thinkers, therefore, the message was the same – religion was outmoded, and had no useful role to play.

A final major influence in the distrust and rejection of religion has been the impact of major warfare and disasters especially in the twentieth and early twenty-first centuries. This has had several strands to it. The impact of two world wars upon some people's theological understanding or the world – their world-view – was profound. 'Where is God in all of this?' is an example of a big 'Why?' question which many people asked and found their faith and theology lacking. The impact of the holocaust had repercussions not just for Jewish theology and post-holocaust theologians, but for many more people whose religious understanding could not accommodate such atrocities. The level of violence in Israel/Palestine causes many people to ask similar questions. Equally daunting has been the development of fundamentalist regimes and contemporary 'crusades' in the name of Islam, for example. Despite strenuous attempts to dissociate the heart of Islam from these political excesses, and to seek to avoid Islamaphobia wherever possible, the impact of these events cannot be under-estimated. Groups of militants continue to do what they have done since time immemorial, and have called upon the name of their 'God' to support them in their territorial imperialism. There are many other points throughout the world where the religions involved may be different, but the issue remains fundamentally the same: imperialism with a religious cloak. And it is the poor and the dispossessed, the refugee and the homeless who are the helpless victims.

These large issues deserve detailed debate and discussion, and it is hoped that readers of this book will want to follow them up. It is not appropriate to attempt a response within this chapter, because unavoidably that would simply be this author's response. It is important that people find their own responses to these issues. The key point to make at this stage is that these large global issues are part of the 'case against' religion and spirituality, and somehow need to be acknowledged and taken seriously, whatever our individual 'take' on them may be.

This has been recognised in some of the contemporary discussions on these themes. In Henery's discussion on spirituality and the return of religion (2003, p. 1106) he draws on the work of Giddens (1991) and Bauman (1997) to explore these themes. Religion is seen as one response to the 'existentially troubling' phenomenon of modernity:

> Such anxiety may become particularly acute when individuals find themselves facing those phenomena that the abstract systems of modernity exclude from ordinary life

– 'madness, criminality; sickness and death; sexuality; and nature'. (Giddens p. 156) Religions, however, provide conceptual and moral resources more able to assuage such anxiety. (Henery 2003, p. 1107)

It is worth noting in passing that the list cited in the above passage contains much of the daily 'bread and butter' issues which face human services practitioners in their daily caseloads.

Bauman explores issues of consumerism, and argues that a modern sense of self-identity is inextricably linked with what we buy and the range of products which we choose to surround us. In this sense 'we are what we buy', and the bewildering range of choices allows us to express our individuality, and 'to play the game'. Not that everyone can 'play the game' of course – that requires resources which are not available to everyone. Bauman argues that religion, especially in its fundamentalist forms, is a threat to this consumerism upon which much of modern capitalism depends, because it provides 'a supposed remedy for a sense of individual incapacity provoked by the consumer society' (*cited in* Henery, 2003, p. 1108). With a deft tweak to George Bernard Shaw's infamous apothegm, we might now proclaim with tongue in cheek, following Bauman's analysis, that 'those who can, buy; those who can't, turn to religion'. As Henery notes:

> Religion is a threat to consumer capitalism because it takes people 'out of the game'. Its truths are static and unchanging and therefore incompatible with a continually revisable environment of knowledge. The conduct and lifestyle it promotes does not emphasise a lifestyle of product acquisition . . . Religion threatens modernity and consumer capitalism by allowing people to opt out of these demands, and – worse – provides a form of communal legitimation for such a choice. (p. 1108)

This provides a fascinating contrast with the position taken by Weber and his argument about the role of religion in the rise of capitalism. Certainly there are many who belong to faith-based organisations, and not just fundamentalists, who would espouse this critique of capitalism and point to the social injustices of global poverty to question the morality of accelerating consumerism. The point to note at this stage of the discussion, however, is the alleged role of religion to provide comfort to those who cannot 'hack it' in a fast-moving society.

Alongside these wider issues however is a cluster of other topics which must be taken seriously in such a debate. Each of them may be seen as a damning indictment against religion, particularly when viewed from a social care perspective with its distinctive value base for celebrating diversity.

The role of women

The role of women is the first of these deep issues. There are several strands to this theme. First, in the various holy books which serve as the authoritative baseline for the three main religions we are exploring in this section – the Torah and the Talmud for Jews; the Bible for Christians; the Qu'ran for Muslims – the role of women is frequently stated as being subservient to men. This has had profound repercussions for family life; for women's freedom to make decisions about their bodies; and for political power and authority. With some notable exceptions, the world of religion is still male-dominated, and the sexism which exists in society generally is seen to be even stronger within many faith communities.

Undoubtably there is now a serious attempt being made by feminist theologians to distinguish between the true heart of each of these religions, in which women enjoy equal status and dignity, and the gendered nature of the holy books and the traditions which have bolstered male dominance down the centuries. Some parts of the Christian church have now accepted women priests and ministers, but resistance to this is still very deep-seated.

Human sexuality

One issue which continues to cause consternation is the way in which the major religions by and large continue to deny the validity of same-sex relationships, and actively ostracise gay and lesbian people from their congregations. Again, the holy books are used to justify this position, and it is an issue which is often characterised by a crusading vehemence. Nevertheless, there are many examples of gay Christian clergy continuing to exercise their leadership role, but the comfort zone for them is very slender, and many gay people involved in faith communities are still afraid to 'come out' for fear of reprisals and rejection.

It is clear that on both of these issues the fundamental value base of social care in its celebrating of diversity is at odds with much traditional teaching on these issues within these faith communities.

Incidents of abuse

One further nail in the coffin of religion as far as many people is concerned are the examples of abuse or inappropriate behaviour within faith communities. The various cases of sexual abuse against children by religious leaders, some of which have been covered up for decades, causes scandal and outrage amongst the population at large. Some of the child abuse scandals have had religious overtones to them. The Victoria Climbié enquiry, for example, revealed that a pastoral leader had 'diagnosed' demon possession and had not notified the authorities of the abuse; and the account of social work supervision including prayer and bible study caused shock and dismay to the profession at large.

Proselytising

There is also a legitimate concern that workers who have a religious allegiance may use opportunities which arise in their work as human services practitioners to seek to persuade vulnerable people to adopt their worker's religious point of view. Although such conduct is clearly forbidden in codes of conduct, this remains an area of concern for some that workers who belong to faith communities may not be scrupulous in working within these guidelines.

Overview

The 'case against' religion as outlined briefly above is powerful in many people's minds. The examples given illustrate that religion and spirituality are powerful forces – they are not the harmless pastimes which some people claim – they can indeed at times be powerful and destructive, and an example (some would argue) of the old tag 'corruptio optimi pessima' – 'take something which is essentially good, and corrupt it or use it for ignoble ends, and the outcome is the worst possible that you can imagine'.

Against this backcloth it is easy to see how issues of religion and spirituality have at very least been ignored on many training syllabuses, and have been seen by practitioners across a wide spectrum as being irrelevant, pathological or even dangerous.

Chapter 3
Religion: The Case For

Again it is important to stress that this is not a forum in which the claims for or against religion, or any particular truth-claims which are made for a particular religion, will be assessed, or for that matter discussed in detail. These will be issues about which the individual reader will have to come to a judgement.

The purpose of this section is to lay down some of the issues which argue in favour of taking religion and spirituality seriously within the field of social care generally. Within this chapter also is some discussion of the work of theorists who may not have themselves espoused a religious approach to life, but whose work in our opinion provides some interesting possible links with the discourse of religion and spirituality. Some of the points are of a general nature; others are much more specific. This section also includes what has been called the 'legislative imperative' which lays a formal requirement upon human services practitioners to take these issues seriously in certain aspects of their work.

Some theoretical perspectives

Before looking at these points, however, it is worth exploring some of the theoretical contributions to the discussion. Without doubt, the work of Weber occupies a central position in the theoretical understanding of the role of religion in society. He studied and wrote extensively about religion, including studies of ancient Judaism, Hinduism, and Buddhism, as well as Christianity. His famous study *The Protestant Ethic and the Spirit of Capitalism*, published in 1904, adopted a different approach from Feuerbach and Marx in that Weber believed that religion could be seen as a positive and creative force for social change. Indeed, he argued that the values deriving from the Protestant Christian world-view provided a core motivation to the economic transformation of the West. In a nutshell, the drive to succeed materially was a desire to serve God, and material success was evidence of divine favour (Giddens, 2001, pp. 536ff; Haralambos *et al.*, 2000, pp. 448ff).

Weber also emphasised the potential revolutionary nature of Christianity in challenging and seeking to overthrow unjust social structures (Giddens, 2001, p. 539), although there is always the concomitant risk that armed struggles conducted from religious motives can be particularly oppressive.

The role which religion – or at least religious organisations – might occupy within society has also been highlighted by some political theorists, albeit indirectly. The work of Etzioni (1995), for example, and the rise of the concept of communitarianism has had significant impact upon British society in recent decades. Here the emphasis has been not only to challenge the individualism encouraged by the Conservative Government, particularly under Margaret Thatcher. It has also sought to develop a society where social welfare is regarded as a positive strength, and where a variety of community groups as well as individuals have a key role to play. With governments increasingly feeling overloaded in their ability to pay for and deliver a range of public services, the role of religious organisations has been brought to the forefront of the debate. As in America, faith communities in Britain and in Europe are beginning to be seen as key players in the provision of services to the community (see Smith, 2001; Harris *et al.*, 2003; Halman and Pettersson, 2001, for example).

This development has been highlighted indirectly by the work of Habermas (1973) who explored the issues of 'legitimation' facing many contemporary governments. Put starkly, Habermas notes that governments are finding it increasingly difficult to resource the welfare programmes demanded by their electorates. But, in turning to the private sector for funding initiatives, they are finding that the clash between public service and profit is creating a resistance to the generation of adequate resources. If the private sector *won't* pay and the government *can't* pay, it is the government who ends up the loser as its credibility with the electorate to deliver its promises is undermined. In this potential vacuum, faith communities are being encouraged to develop an increasingly active role as the provider of welfare services within their communities. Issues of doctrinal truth mean little in this context: if a faith community can deliver the goods, they will get the contract.

These wider political contexts are important to the discussion inasmuch as they set the scene for ways in which faith communities are becoming increasingly recognised as key players in community regeneration and development.

Another theorist who deserves some attention at this point is Ulrich Beck, who is perhaps best known for his writings around a 'risk society'. For Beck, 'the management of risk is the prime feature of global order' (Giddens, 2001, p. 678), which is marked by new risks posed by the development of science and technology – the debate about the 'risks' of genetically modified crops is an example of this. Beck also reflects on the ways in which risk calculations characterise the making and sustaining of relationships when divorce rates are high: 'The individual must judge his or her likelihood of securing happiness and security against this backdrop' (Giddens, p. 678).

This analysis of the 'risk society' can work in two ways, of course. For some, there is an added frisson of excitement and challenge as they move through uncharted waters. New forms of political pressure groups emerge to challenge the view that decisions about the future of society can safely be left in the hands of the politicians. Within the framework of spirituality suggested in this book – that spirituality is what we do to express our chosen world-view – there is clearly plenty of scope for people to develop new patterns of meaning and purpose. The bewildering rise of 'new age' religious movements may be understood against the background of this increasingly risk-filled society; indeed, it is possible to view risk as a positive and creative opportunity, and maybe for some a prophetic challenge to traditional political structures.

For others, by contrast, there is an increased sense of unease in a 'risk society' which can push them towards those faith communities which offer a deeper sense of security, meaning and purpose in life. For them religion remains perhaps something more akin to the 'haven from the storm' which Marx critiqued so long ago. In an uncertain, risky world, many people actively seek and are hugely relieved to find organisations which offer a sense of security which they believe both outlasts and underpins an otherwise transient society. This would explain the rise of fundamentalism within both Christianity and Islam, and its increasing popularity.

It is of course of vital importance that people come to a view about the truth-claims of the organisations – including the faith communities – which they join, and which best reflect their chosen world-view. The significance for our discussion on religion and spirituality is that there is a resonance with some key political science theorists which it is important to recognise if we are to appreciate the role which religion and spirituality play within contemporary society.

Some further theoretical developments are worth noting in the field of social psychology. The work of Maslow (1962) will be familiar to students across a range of disciplines, not least because of his now famous theory about a 'hierarchy of needs'. This asserts that human beings have a range of needs, from the basic physiological needs such as hunger, thirst and sex; and safety needs such as avoidance of pain and need for security; then a sense of belonging and intimacy; then esteem needs such as self respect, until finally he places self-actualisation at the peak at which point humans can fulfil their true potential, and strive for justice and creativity. Maslow suggests that people can only reach the final stages when they have had the lower levels of need satisfied.

Leaving to one side for a moment a critique of Maslow's theory – quite where hunger strikes and self-sacrifice fit into his schema is not clear, for example – it does at least have some scope for locating spirituality within the self-actualisation set of 'higher' needs. It must be said, however, that to deny access to such meaning-making until the higher level of needs is reached runs the risk of compartmentalising spirituality, or limiting it to what Maslow referred to as 'peak experiences' or intense mystical moments of feeling connected to other people. This contrasts with some existentialist perspectives which argue, for example, that suffering is a necessary part of human growth (Hutchison, 2003, p. 81). Here there is a strong link with both religious and some spiritual traditions which seek to find meaning to what is sometimes called the 'problem of suffering'. Christianity and Hinduism have contrasting approaches to this, but both recognise that this is a significant part of the human condition which somehow has to be located within a framework of meaning-making, which we have suggested is at the heart of what spirituality is all about. Here again we see possible links between psychological theory and religion and spirituality.

Generally speaking, in a range of helping professions including nursing and social work, there has been an increasing emphasis upon a holistic approach to care, emphasising the needs of the whole person. However, as Canda and Smith (2003) point out:

> They have usually emphasised the biological, psychological and social dimensions of personhood while minimising spirituality. (p. 6)

A lot of work has been done in America to explore ways in which a more holistic approach could be developed which could include spirituality. Transpersonal psychology represents a serious, albeit complex, attempt to achieve this greater synthesis, by offering an approach to human behaviour which includes levels of consciousness which move beyond the rational individualised ego to a wider understanding of the self:

> First foreseen by Maslow (1971) as an emerging 'Fourth Force' psychology of transcendence, transpersonalism is an inclusive theory that adds spirituality into mainstream psychology. Transpersonal practice thus seeks to assess and foster not only the spiritual, but also the cognitive, emotional, physical, and social dimensions of development. (Derezotes, 2001, p. 164)

A further comment illustrates the point:

> Transpersonal functioning allows us to transcend identification with roles, possessions, status, wealth and other attachments so that we can experience peace of mind and connection with our souls and the universe. (Derezotes, 2001, p. 168)

There is not the opportunity in this book fully to describe, let alone debate this approach and its relevance to human service work (for a critique, see Hutchison, 2003, pp. 246 ff). The point to make is that, within mainstream psychology there is a contemporary movement to take religion and spirituality seriously by exploring new theoretical models which seek to incorporate these dimensions and relate them to a range of practice situations.

One further example is the development of resilience theory. At first glance this may seem to have nothing to do with religion and spirituality, and instead everything to do with empowering and enabling emotionally hurt and damaged children to survive a variety of traumatic and abusive experiences. This is captured well by Gilligan (1997) who defines resilience as involving:

> Qualities which cushion a vulnerable child from the worst effects of adversity in whatever form it takes and which may help a child or young person to cope, survive

and even thrive in the face of great hurt and disadvantage. (p. 12, cited in Daniel *et al.*, 1999)

An important point in this from the child's perspective is highlighted by Rutter (1999; 2000). In describing the factors that are important for psychologically healthy adult development, he observes that it is important for young people:

to accept the reality of the bad experiences they have had, and to find a way of incorporating the reality of these experiences into their own self-concept, but doing so in a way that builds on the positive while not denying the negative. (p. 135)

If instead of 'self-concept' we talk about 'world-view' we are close to the territory being explored for spirituality.

Another underlying principle here also has clear links with aspects of religion and spirituality. This involves the recognition that, at their best, religion and spirituality can both recognise and release power and potential within people to transcend experiences of great pain and loss. We often refer to the idea of 'rising above' the problems and traumas which can happen to us. In this sense we can understand the positive and enabling aspects of religion and spirituality as both nurturing and releasing within people a greater resilience to cope with life in its darkest moments.

Again, there is no space within this discussion for a more detailed critique of resilience theory. The point to make, however, is that this is another example where it is possible to make creative links with a theoretical perspective which enables us to take seriously the positive contribution which religion and spirituality can make to people's lives. It may also be that there is a creative link between some aspects of religion and spirituality, resilience theory and anti-discriminatory, anti-oppressive, emancipatory practice. This is a possibility to which we will return in the third part of this book.

Religion: the case for – some more general points

1. There can be no denying that interest in religion generally, and membership of faith communities in particular, is still strong world wide. A recent estimate of people belonging to faith communities within the UK is as follows:

According to 'Religious Trends 1998/99' there are over 20,000 Christian churches, over 600 Muslim groups, over 200 Sikh groups, around 200 Buddhist groups, over 150 Hindu groups and over 350 Jewish groups in the United Kingdom. (Smith, 1999, s. 1.1, p. 1)

According to the 2001 Census for England and Wales, there are 37.3 million people in England and Wales who state their religion as Christian. 3.1 per cent state their religion as Muslim (source: Census 2001 – Ethnicity and religion in England and Wales: http://www.statistics.gov.uk/cci/nugget.asp?id = 293).

At the very least this indicates that we are not dealing with a marginalised activity, but that religion still is a major force within the world.

2. There is evidence that, although some of the mainstream Christian churches in the UK are in decline, other religions are showing an increase in interest. Black Majority Churches, for example, have a membership of approximately 100,000 in the UK (Patel, 1998, p. 25). The issue of membership is of course problematic, with some religious groups operating strict criteria for joining, whilst others reflect a wider cultural sense of belonging. Figures suggested in 1997 (Weller, 1997 – cited in Patel, 1998, p. 23) for the main faith communities in the UK, as defined in the broadest sense, are as follows :

Baha'is	6000
Buddhists	30,000–130,000
Christians	40,000,000
Hindus	400,000–550,000
Jains	25,000–30,000
Jews	300,000
Muslims	1,000,000–1,500,000
Sikhs	350,000–500,000
Zoroastrians	5,000–10,000

Weller (2004) offers a detailed discussion of some of the issues arising from the UK Census 2001, especially about the differences in emphasis in Northern Ireland and Scotland. Three quarters of the UK population reported having a religion, with 72 per cent claiming to be Christian (37.3 million), and 3 per cent Muslim (1.6 million).

These figures suggest that there is a significant proportion of the population of the UK for whom issues of religion and spirituality are important.

3. There seems to be an increase in issues to do with spirituality as evidenced by the growth of interest in non-traditional religious activities.

4. Many religious communities are harnessing a lot of energy and commitment serving not just their local communities in the fight against poverty and social exclusion, but also on a larger world wide canvas with anti-poverty work and political lobbying on behalf of political prisoners.

5. Faith communities undertake a significant amount of pastoral and caring work within their local communities, including work with young people, families, unemployed people and older people. They continue to offer pastoral care to people at the end of their lives and through times of bereavement and sickness.

6. Some sections of the multicultural communities in the UK not only positively identify with their faith communities, but also see them as an important network and resource against the racism of the wider community. The role of faith communities in consolidating and celebrating cultural identities is significant.

7. Many faith communities are in the vanguard of multicultural developments within local communities to help build greater tolerance and mutual respect

between groups. Some actively encourage their members to play an active part in local politics for the benefit of their communities.

8. Many multi-faith communities play a lead role in developing a wide range of cultural activities in their local areas.

9. There are examples of faith-based organisations (FBOs) undertaking specific projects to improve the quality of life for the whole community of which they are part. They play a role in developing social capital and in raising and tackling social justice concerns within their local communities (Smith, 1999).

10. FBOs still have a role to play within education at local and national levels, and are consulted by government on a range of issues of national and international concern. They also from time to time challenge government policy, and seek to provide moral leadership and guidance.

11. Some research is beginning to emerge which suggests some positive correlations between religious faith/belonging to a faith community and psychological well-being (Swinton, 2001, pp. 68–71). Some of these issues are explored further in Part Three.

This kaleidoscope of activities illustrates the wealth of resources available in local communities through faith-based organisations, much of which goes unacknowledged and unsung, although some research into this is now beginning to be undertaken (for example, Farnell *et al.*, 2003). It is not to suggest, however, that these are the only care activities which happen in local communities, or that people who do not belong to faith communities do not also actively participate in such work – far from it. It is simply to make the point that FBOs do contribute positively and creatively and significantly to society at all levels, and deserve for that reason, if for no other, to be taken seriously by human services practitioners.

Finally, it is not inappropriate to reflect on the ways in which religious and spiritual convictions have played a significant part in the development of many of the social care agencies which are now part of the fabric of our society – although admittedly 'for the social work profession in the west, the impact of Christianity on social work has become a barely remembered part of the professional heritage' (Bowpitt, 1998, p. 676).

Nevertheless, much of the early impetus towards social work came from religiously motivated philanthropy. The origins of the Probation Service, once committed to 'advise, assist and befriend', may be found in the 'Police Court Missionaries' who 'loitered creatively' at the magistrates' courts in order to help and guide those who had fallen foul of the criminal law. These became probation officers in 1907, 'although it was many years before the statutory probation service disentangled itself from its religious and voluntary roots' (Williams, 1995, p. 23). The strong religious convictions of many probation officers may be evidenced by the fact that prayers were only dropped from the annual general meeting of the National Association of Probation Officers after bitter arguments in the late 1970s (Williams, 1995, p. 41).

Some of the foundational principles of social work, counselling, and the active listening skills which have now permeated much professional practice, may be traced to the work of Biestek (1957), who was himself a Roman Catholic priest. Faith communities have pioneered work with young people, whilst the role of chaplains within hospitals has long been an accepted feature of medical life.

This brief snapshot illustrates the wealth of resources available to local communities through their FBOs, the potential for which still has fully to be realised.

Chapter 4
Legislative Imperatives

It is time to turn specifically to aspects of legislation which place religion and spirituality on the agenda as far as human services practitioners are concerned. This is not to say of course that these will be at the top of any list of concerns, or that their importance is being overemphasised. Rather, it is an acknowledgement that these issues deserve to be taken seriously if holistic assessments are to be made, and if the full range of needs is to be taken into account. What it should ensure is that issues of religion and spirituality are considered properly and fully alongside all the other dimensions of human service care, and that it is not left to the individual whim or preference of the professional, supervisor, assessor or manager as to whether these issues are raised or not. Put starkly, these imperatives should ensure that best practice appropriately and professionally includes religion and spirituality across the whole spectrum of professional care.

For the purposes of this section of the book, legislation has been used in a very loose sense in that it will include material contained in, for example, United Nation Conventions, and in guidance and regulation documents. The following list is not meant to be exhaustive, but rather to illustrate a range of areas where it has been clearly stated that issues of religion and spirituality need to be considered.

The Human Rights Act 1998

Article 9 of the Human Rights Act 1998 deals with freedom of thought, conscience and religion, and states:

1. *Everyone has the right to freedom of thought, conscience and religion; this right includes freedom to change his [sic] religion or belief, and freedom either alone or in community with others and in public or private, to manifest his religion or belief, in worship, teaching, practice and observance.*
2. *Freedom to manifest one's religion of beliefs shall be subject only to such limitations as are prescribed by law and are necessary in a democratic society in the interest of public safety, for the protection of public order, health or morals, or for the protection of the rights and freedoms of others.*

The implications of the Human Rights Act are far reaching, and can impact upon every aspect of a human services practitioner's work. To take these two sections seriously lays a heavy burden of responsibility upon the worker first of all to recognise that the issues of religion and spirituality are important. The demands of best practice mean that workers must be willing to take the initiative and test out the extent to which these issues are important to the people with whom they are working. Secondly, human services practitioners must respond sensitively and appropriately when such issues are brought onto the agenda, whether this is on behalf of a 'looked-after' child or a person approaching the end of life in a hospital or hospice; a person struggling to find meaning and purpose in their life, or someone in residential care who has a variety of religious and spiritual needs; a person whose offending behaviour tempts the worker to regard them as a failure as a human being and fit only for punishment or incarceration, or someone who wishes to celebrate their disability beneath the rainbow of diversity.

The examples of a legislative imperative given below are far from exhaustive, but seek to illustrate how these issues are being taken seriously, and present important challenges to the human services worker.

The Children Act 1989

Section 22(4) discusses the decisions with respect to 'looked-after children' and requires a local authority, so far as is reasonably practicable, to ascertain the wishes and feelings of the child, the parents, any person who has parental responsibility or anyone else deemed by the authority to have a relevant contribution to make:

> In making any such decision a local authority shall give due consideration to . . . the child's religious persuasion, racial origin and cultural and linguistic background.

This is acknowledged in the *Framework for the Assessment of Children in Need and their Families* (DoH, 2000), where it is stated that:

> The Children Act 1989 is built on the premise that . . . differences in bringing up children due to family structures, *religion*, culture and ethnic origins *should be respected and understood.* (s. 1.42 p. 12, emphasis added)

However, scant attention is paid to these issues in the document itself, where the diagrammatic Assessment Framework triangle (pp. 17 and 89), for example, makes no mention of religion and spirituality at all.

In the guidance and regulations for The Children Act 1989 there are additional important references. For example, in *Volume 3: Family Placements*, the following sections mention religious or spiritual issues:

s.2 42–49	religious background
2.62	religious needs as a key element in a placement plan
4.4–5	continuity in religious/church life
8.20	on religious provision in review

See Dept. of Health circular LAC(98)20 paragraphs 11–18 for further details.

In *Volume 4: Residential Care*, the following sections are relevant:

1.121–124   religious observance
1.153   provision for religious items in records
2.21   identifying appropriate religious provision
2–62   identified religious needs as a key element of a placement plan
2.81   religious certificates
3.19   religious provision in review
7.46   religion of befriender
7.53   counselling and religious matching

The Adoption and Children Act 2002 (not fully implemented until 2004) also states that an adoption agency placing a child for adoption must give due consideration to a child's religion, race, language and culture.

It is worth noting at this point that, in The Department of Health's studies in evaluating the Children Act 1989 (DoH, 2001a), some key lessons were drawn out of 12 overview reports by the Social Services Inspectorate on services for children and families. The focus of attention was on the ways in which the four key Children Act principles – promoting the welfare of the child; having regard for the child's wishes and feelings; working in partnership; and meeting children's specific needs – had been implemented. They found that: 'The area requiring most work was that of meeting specific needs (with respect to race, *religion*, disability etc.)' (p. 247, emphasis added).

United Nations Convention on the Rights of the Child 1989

This was ratified by the UK Government in 1991, and contains various references to religious and spiritual rights. Several key points outlined below give the flavour of how religious and spiritual issues are tackled, but for more detailed discussion see for example Crompton (1998), Bradford (1995) and Nurnberg (1995).

Preamble, para 3.
The United Nations has, in the Universal Declaration of Human Rights and in the International Covenants on Human Rights, proclaimed and agreed that everyone is entitled to all the rights and freedoms set forth therein, without distinction of any kind, such as race, colour, sex, language, religion, political or other opinion, national or social origin, property, birth or other status, in suitable institutions for the care of children. When considering solutions, due regard shall be paid to the desirability of continuity in a child's upbringing and to the child's ethnic, religious, cultural and spiritual background.
14   respect the right of the child to freedom of thought, conscience and religion

14.1   freedom to manifest one's religion or beliefs may be subject only to such limitations as are prescribed by law and are necessary to protect public safety, order, health or morals, or the fundamental rights and freedoms of others.

30.   in those States in which ethnic, religious or linguistic minorities of persons of indigenous origin exist, a child belonging to such a minority or who is indigenous shall not be denied the right, in community with other members of his or her group, to enjoy his or her own culture, to profess and practise his or her own religion, or to use his or her own language.

2.   ensure that the child is protected against all forms of discrimination or punishment on the basis of the status, activities, expressed opinions, or beliefs of the child's parents, guardians or family members

29.   prepare the child for responsible life in a free society, in the spirit of understanding, peace, equality of the sexes, and friendship among all peoples, ethnic, national and religious groups and persons of indigenous origin.

Crime and Disorder Act 1998

The Crime and Disorder Act 1998 has some important contributions to make to the discussion about the nature of racial attacks against minority groups. The issues are complex in that some careful unravelling is often needed for issues of race and religion. One key issues here is the Home Office guidance regarding racially aggravated offences. It states that it is important to investigate whether an offence, which may appear to be motivated by religious hostility also contains a racist element. Provided that part of the religious hostility is racist then a racist offence will have occurred (http://www.crimereduction.gov.uk/toolkits/rh0203.htm).

The principal issue here concerns race, rather than religious affiliation. For many people, however, these 'boundaries' are blurred – indeed, the very notion of boundaries in these matters is alien to many: Muslims, Sikhs and Jews, for example. Some interesting case law is worth citing to show how the law has regarded an 'ethnic group'. Lord Fraser held, for example, that Sikhs did constitute an 'ethnic group', and outlined some of the characteristics needed, including a long, shared history; a cultural tradition and a common language or literature, or *a common religion different from neighbouring groups* (emphasis added – source: Mandla v Dowell Lee 1983 1 All ER 1062).

The employment equality (religion or belief) regulations 2003

These regulations make it unlawful to discriminate on the grounds of religion or belief in employment and vocational training. This is to comply with the EC Equal

Treatment Framework Directive. These regulations are intended to include not just the so-called 'mainstream' religions but also include other belief systems such as paganism and humanism.

As always there are two aspects to such regulations. They say clearly what should not happen. But there is also the issue about best practice towards which such regulations point employers. These can include a sensitivity to the need for prayer room facilities and the observance of religious festivals, and the timing of meetings to avoid religious commitments.

Overview

This brief summary of what we have called the 'legislative imperatives' have revealed some significant issues. First, there is no doubt that religion and spirituality are recognised as being important, and deserve to be taken seriously across a wide range of professional human service settings. Second, it is one thing to claim such importance: it is quite another to take these issues seriously enough to embed them into practice. Third, it is likely that there is still something of an 'engagement gap' between the language of spirituality and the realities to which the concept seeks to point. As Crompton (1998) observes:

> Spirituality is not a commodity for measurement or testing; there is no examination which can be passed or failed, or one approved language of communication. (p. 37)

In other words, the big 'So what?' question is raised starkly: all this talk of religion and spirituality is all very well, but so what? Exactly how can I begin to address these issues in my practice? If best practice is supposed to include an acknowledgement of religious and/or spiritual issues, how do I go about it?

It is these practice issues that Part Two will address.

Part Two: Implications for Practice

Introduction

In Part One the issues of religion and spirituality were discussed and put into context. It was acknowledged that religion in particular can be both a positive and negative influence upon people's lives, and the implications of this important insight will be explored in more detail in Part Three which looks at anti-discriminatory, anti-oppressive and emancipatory practice issues. In this section we will be exploring some of the ways in which religion and spirituality impact upon practice.

From the outset we need to acknowledge that there are two dimensions to this: the practitioner, and the person who uses the services which we offer. Each one of us, whether as service providers or service users – or at times both – will locate ourselves somewhere on what we might for the sake of convenience call the 'spirituality spectrum'. At one end there will be those for whom there is a clear overlap between religion and spirituality through their active participation in a faith community. This will very clearly also establish a value base which they seek to respect and live by. At the other extreme there will be those for whom the concept of spirituality, even as defined in this book as 'what we do to give expression to our chosen world-view', does not sit easily in their thinking, or perhaps even provokes a hostile reaction, for whatever reason. And there will be as many points along this 'spirituality spectrum' as there are people to fill them.

It will be important to focus on both the service provider as well as those who use our services, although it must be admitted that the approach most familiar to professionals will be the latter. In other words, professionals like doctors, nurses, social workers, health workers are familiar with the official documentation which may ask for details of a person's religion. In some instances this will trigger off, perfectly appropriately, a referral to a leader of a faith community whose task will be to explore that person's religious and spiritual needs. Hospital care is a classic example of this, where a lot of work has been done to help staff recognise the importance of religious and spiritual care, especially in patients whose circumstances give rise to serious concern.

The temptation, here, of course is to regard such issues in a compartmentalised way, and to make the assumption that once a referral has been made the matter has been dealt with – for example:

- This patient needs a special diet – it's up to the catering manager to provide it.
- This young person needs an interview for a job – JobCentre Plus or the Connexions Service will sort that out.
- This person needs to learn I.T. skills – there is a course provided locally which will see to that, and it is free – so that is a double bonus which makes us all feel even better about it!
- This person I am counselling seems to have a link with a local faith community, so that lets me off the hook when it comes to talking about such things which I don't know much about anyway.
- I have ticked the box and made a referral to a leader of a faith community, so that is sorted.
- The person has said 'none' to the question about religious affiliation on my form, so we can forget all about that and get on with the real work.

Of course, it is wholly appropriate that we recognise the role of chaplains and faith-community leaders in our multi-faith society. They have relevant expertise, and are comfortable in offering religious and spiritual care, often beyond the boundaries of their own particular faith community. But to restrict religion and spirituality to a narrow box of ecclesiastical conformism is to miss an important point. Muslims are not alone in claiming that their faith is about the whole of life, and that what they believe permeates every aspect of their living. If the definition of spirituality offered in this book rings true – 'spirituality is what we do to give expression to our chosen world-view' – then we should expect that this permeation will occur to a greater or lesser extent with everybody, even if it is not clearly articulated. The world-view and the values which a person chooses to live by illustrate the 'heart and soul' of that person – their 'very being' as some would say – and to operate as human services workers in any field without acknowledging that is to diminish the holistic service which many professionals seek to offer.

This is not to suggest that any one person should attempt to be omnicompetent of course. It is no service to the patient to expect an ear, nose and throat specialist to have a stab at complex brain surgery. There is a vital role for religious leaders to play in caring for people and in dealing with faith and worship issues, and those not trained or familiar with these areas would be doing a disservice to people if they tried to fulfil such a role. The point being made here, however, is not to undermine the role of the faith specialist (if we may use that term), but to stress that such issues can so permeate a person's approach to life that we will be doing them an equal disservice if we do *not* find ways of exploring these issues with them as far as they relate to the service we are seeking to provide.

But we are in danger already of ignoring one major dimension. It is easy to slip into a discussion (as indeed we have just done) about the needs of patients and people who use the services we offer, and to think that somehow, by virtue of being professional, these issues do not concern us. There is a temptation, in other words, to ignore our own spirituality and the impact it has upon our professional work. And for those who have a particular allegiance to a faith community and who seek to live by the values inculcated by that allegiance, there may also be particular issues which need to be explored from their professional perspective. This is an important area to which we must now turn.

Chapter 5
Personal Perspectives

'Me? A spiritual person? You must be joking!'

This perhaps all-too-familiar retort not only illustrates the well-used maxim of the subjects to avoid talking about at dinner parties; it also points up the problems of definitions, which we explored in Part One. Many people lump religion and spirituality together into one untidy heap and, perhaps because of its very untidiness, dismiss it from any serious consideration. The secularisation of contemporary British society perhaps lends itself to this reaction. Religion (with its travelling companion, spirituality) are perceived as being the rag, tag and bobtail of pre-enlightenment days, or the territory of the fundamentalist zealot. On both counts, many would argue, they deserve to be dismissed.

One major task, therefore, which this book seeks to address, is to encourage people to explore a wider definition such as the one we have suggested, and to see that this is an issue which affects each and everyone of us, and is not something which we can relegate to the strange fascination of a minority. We also would argue that the values which derive from our chosen world-view – be they specifically religious, atheistic or less clearly defined – are with us in our professional lives as well as in our private lives, and need to be acknowledged.

In some ways this should not be such strange territory as some may think. In the core training curricula for several professions, for example, it is expected that students will be able to develop the skills of reflective practice as part of their educational and professional development. This not only involves the skills of being able to apply the core underpinning knowledge to practice situations with a developing level of competence; it also involves some other dimensions as well. As indicated in the Introduction to this book, the concept of 'self-location' is of particularly importance here. Put at its simplest, this means that each of us needs to take into account the effect of our race, gender, class, disability upon our professional practice, and how we relate to the people who come to us for help.

To illustrate the point from the standpoint of sociology, we can gain an insight from what is often called a 'feminist' approach to social research. This has involved a critique of 'malestream' research which is seen as being based upon sexist and patriarchal principles, and often excludes the reality of women's experience (Haralambos *et al.*, 2000, p. 987). In other words, whether consciously or unconsciously, men had been allowing their assumptions about women to influence how they had conducted and interpreted their research. It needed women to begin to articulate, and then carry out feminist research in order to *capture* (is this 'male-speak' here?) or do justice to the richness and variety of women's experience. The point being made is clear: research is not gender neutral.

An anecdote from practice provides a further example. Several years ago a male social worker was conducting an assessment on a woman and her children who had escaped from serious and prolonged domestic violence and were living in a women's refuge. It became clear after a while that the male social worker's value base and personal, cultural world-view emphasised the importance of the family staying together at all costs, and this was reflected in his court report recommendations. Fortunately the woman's barrister was able to challenge the report and managed to achieve an outcome which fully protected her and the children. The point of the story is clear: although the professional value base of social work stresses the importance of an even-handed assessment which (in this case) needed to recognise the children's interests and safety being of paramount importance, the male social worker's own value base had been allowed to influence the outcome of the report in an inappropriate way.

In case you think that this was an extreme example, it is worth listing some further examples from practice which illustrate the point. As you read through this list, be aware of your own feelings and opinions about the scenarios being suggested. Your reactions will highlight for you something about your own value base and world-view:

- You are a nurse in a hospice and have to offer physical nursing care to someone with HIV/AIDS.
- You are a youth worker and are aware of young people moving from soft to hard drugs and who want you to help them find work.
- You are a care worker in a residential unit for 'looked-after children' and are aware that several of the young people are having sex under the legal age of consent.
- You are working with two people who have learning difficulties who wish to begin a sexual relationship together.
- You work in an area of high unemployment where asylum seekers come to you for help and advice about finding work.
- You have to prepare a court report on a paedophile.
- A female street worker comes to your advice centre for welfare benefits advice.

This small handful of examples has been suggested not to highlight what our professional and legal responsibilities may be – these are often quite clear – but to help us understand that our own values and world-views are frequently involved in the work which we undertake, and in the practice dilemmas which we face on a regular basis.

We can take the matter further, and into the specific realm of religion and spirituality, with a further set of cameos:

- You are a committed member of a faith community, and a social worker, and are making an assessment about whether or not to recommend a gay couple as potential adopters.
- You work in a medical setting and are faced with cases of male and female circumcision, and wonder if this should be classed as abuse.
- You work in a team where there is a committed Muslim who is claiming the right to have prayer facilities and 'time-out' for prayers during the working day.
- You are working with someone who is about to die and appears supremely confident about an afterlife, whereas you are not only unsure but are quite frightened by the thought of dying.
- You belong to a faith community but feel that members of your team consistently devalue you because of your religious beliefs, and challenge your capacity to work professionally and not to proselytise.
- You are working with a family who claim that it is culturally and religiously acceptable to exercise physical chastisement upon their children.
- You are working in a hospital setting where a family refuse on religious grounds to allow a blood transfusion to be given to their child.
- You belong to a faith community and are working with someone who is terminally ill. They want to discuss what you think happens after people die.

Again, these cameos are to help you reflect on your attitudes about issues to do with religion and spirituality, and the extent to which your own views differ from, or are similar to those with whom we have to work. That is why most of the cameos have not been given a designated role such as a social worker, youth worker, counsellor or nurse, where professional codes of conduct come into play. These cameos are intended to raise our awareness of our personal world-view, our own spirituality and values. In other words, our response tells us something about our own spirituality.

There are of course serious limitations to such an approach. In the professional contexts within which we work there are often clear guidelines, policies and procedures which we are required to follow which may help to alleviate some of the dilemmas we may face. But underlying all of this is the personal professional relationship we strike up with those who come to use the services we offer. Best practice suggests that we do not hide behind the paperwork, however vital the documentation happens to be. Best practice talks about a quality of professional relationship that has an honesty and integrity about it, and which values and respects the dignity of each individual, and the world-view which they have chosen. Within the limits of professional codes of practice, we owe it to those who use the services we offer to be as fully human as we can. And that involves unavoidably – but potentially creatively – our own spirituality; for we too need to be able to make sense and give meaning to the world as we experience it, and as we contribute to its well-being.

Paradoxically, perhaps, the best way of ensuring that we do provide a complete holistic service to people which takes into account issues of religion and spirituality, is to be honest with ourselves about where we are coming from. If we as workers can appropriately locate ourselves in matters to do with religion and spirituality, it will help us not only to keep these issues 'on the agenda', but will ensure that we begin to do justice to the other person's experience.

Working with others

In Part One we gave some attention to some of the legislative imperatives which underpin much of the work which we do. The reason for this was to remind us that these issues of religion and spirituality are not a matter of personal whim or enthusiasm: they belong in the mainstream of practice, and we owe it to the people with whom we work to deal with these matters appropriately.

When it comes to exploring exactly how this might happen, we are faced with a variety of possible approaches which could be adopted in this chapter. We could, for example, simply itemise a large number of scenarios across several professions where religion and spirituality might be legitimately raised and discussed. Individual readers could then select the scenarios which seemed to be of greatest interest. Or, we could adopt an approach which selects certain religious and spiritual perspectives, and use these as templates to hold across a range of work-based scenarios to highlight particular issues. We could look at issues from a Christian or Muslim or atheistic point of view, for example, to illustrate how these issues might work in practice. That there is scope for such approaches may be illustrated from the work being done in the United States, for example (Scales *et al.*, 2002).

A further approach might be to focus on particular aspects of human services work and explore the implications for religion and spirituality. Such an approach could look at issues around mental health; work with children or elders; issues to do with disability or socially excluded groups. Each of these – and many more – would provide great scope for detailed discussion, and would be of interest to particular subject specialists.

Each of these approaches could enrich our understanding and practice across a range of disciplines. For the purposes of this chapter, however, a more modest approach has been adopted whereby some key themes have been identified which span most if not all the disciplines which will be interested in this topic. With each theme an attempt will be made in an introductory way to explore the links with religion and spirituality to encourage people to see the possible connections, and where these issues have particular relevance. The discussion will not be exhaustive, but illustrative: a 'starter for ten' rather than a definitive conclusion.

The three main themes chosen for this discussion are:

1. the loss of meaning and the meaning of loss;
2. forgiveness; and
3. social justice.

Chapter 6
The Loss of Meaning and the Meaning of Loss

The somewhat 'snappy' title for this chapter brings us face to face with an aspect of life which is far from 'snappy'. Loss is, without doubt, one of the biggest themes of human existence, and penetrates the work of human service practitioners at every turn. It would be comforting perhaps to be able to say that just because it is such a mainstream feature of human living we have developed robust practical and emotional strategies for dealing with such issues when they arise. But we all know that many of us haven't!

Behind all the labels we wear, the gut-wrenching heartache of real loss hits us all and knocks us sideways. The university professor, and the newest student; the NHS consultant and the anxious patient; the nursing sister and youngest recruit; the hospital porter and the person being pushed along on the trolley; the dynamic youth worker and the painfully insecure young person; the experienced counsellor and the person struggling to express their feelings, the social worker who 'has seen it all' and the service user who is having to 'live it all'; the faith community leader and the person coming for spiritual guidance; the debt adviser and the person with a sackful of unpaid bills – each and every one of us, wherever we find ourselves in the complex tapestry of our community, is likely to feel devastated when experiencing profound loss. However well prepared we think we may be, it seems to be the case that even the best preparations we make can only be at best a moderately strong sea wall which ultimately the crashing waves will breach.

This is not meant to sound gloomy and pessimistic. It is meant to be honest and realistic. And more importantly, it is intended to express something profoundly significant about being human, and puts us in touch with the whole issue of spirituality and what gives meaning and purpose to our lives. It is precisely *because* we have the capacity to love that the loss of a loved one hurts so much. Gibran (1926) caught this in his meditation on sorrow and joy: 'When you are sorrowful, look again into your heart, and you shall see that in truth you are weeping for that which has been your delight' (p. 36).

Arthur Quiller Couch (1923) caught something of the reality of this when he described grief as: 'The unwelcome lodger that squats on the hearth between us and the fire, and will not move or be dislodged'.

It is not surprising that literary references start tumbling over each other when this theme is mentioned: its sheer universality strikes a chord in us all.

The significance for our discussion lies not just in the sharp experiences of bereavement, but in the all-embracing domain of loss. Whether it is in the loss of identity and self-confidence; the loss of employment or of a partner through separation or divorce; the loss of physical capacity or mental acuity; the loss of opportunity through a particular 'failure' – loss strikes at us all. It is no wonder that it is precisely at these times that our sense of meaning, purpose and direction can also take a battering, especially if it was a bit shaky before.

How often in the news bulletins which accompany major disasters do we hear newscasters commenting that 'the people involved are struggling *to come to terms with* what has happened to them'. The greater the loss, the harder this challenge will feel, and it must be openly acknowledged that for many people the gaping chasm left in their lives by a major trauma may never be filled. They may spend the rest of their lives learning how to walk round it with a hesitating familiarity, but the gaping void will never be filled. Anniversaries tear the scab off the emotional wounds; familiar music brings memories flooding back. The walk past the place where you used to work re-kindles the ache if not always the anger. Seeing your children happily settled with a new partner brings pangs of guilt about the parenting you can no longer fully provide. Like Gruyere cheese or the pitted lunar landscape, the painful holes become part of our personality whether we like it or not, and the big question hits us : 'what sense can we make of this to enable us to carry on with our lives with some modicum of success and enjoyment?' Or, as Morgan (1993) puts it: 'how can you make sense out of a world which does not seem to be intrinsically reasonable?' (p. 6).

It is at this point that human services practitioners perfectly reasonably ask for some help from theoretical perspectives and research findings to help them deal with these major issues of loss. In the first instance they ask this question in order better to be able to provide best practice for those who come to them for help and support. But there is a bonus in this: the theoretical frameworks offer help and encouragement to the worker every bit as much as to those who come to them for professional support. Furthermore, if as workers we can have some real insight into these issues in our own lives, then it is likely that it will increase our sensitivity to those people also experiencing loss with whom we are seeking to work. And in terms of the specific topics of this book, we will find that, perhaps to our surprise, we are in the mainstream of the discussion about spirituality, if not religion itself. For the responses (it's a bit optimistic to expect answers) which people give to these profoundly disturbing and challenging questions posed by serious loss are ultimately spiritual, in that they uncover the particular world-view which people have chosen to underpin their lives.

It may be of course that this chosen world-view proves to be profoundly lacking when the litmus test of deep loss is applied to it. This then increases a person's emotional 'angst' as they seek to find another world-view which can encompass what their loss has forced them to acknowledge. Painful though the process may be both for the person and the professional helper who may be caught up with them in it all, it need not be viewed in a negative light completely. Crisis intervention theory has taught us to view such 'upheaval moments' as potential opportunities to re-think and re-shape our lives and our priorities (Thompson, 1991). It provides an opportunity for the person involved and the professionals who are working with them to acknowledge this dimension, and not to run away from exploring it, however tempting that might be.

The recent developments in our understanding and appreciation of dealing with loss within the context of bereavement and death-related losses have implications for many other loss experiences. Of the several important theoretical strands to emerge, two in particular deserve mention. The first is 'meaning re-construction' theory; the second is the 'dual process' model (for a detailed introduction, see Thompson 2002a, pp. 1–22). Both approaches may be seen to have a spiritual and religious dimension to them, although neither of them specifically addresses these perspectives in any depth.

Before looking at these two models, however, it is worth saying something about the 'received wisdom' of the 'stages of grief' model which still dominates the theoretical understanding of many human services practitioners who were brought up on the work of Kübler-Ross and others. It probably says more about those who cling rigidly to the stages model than about those who first offered it as a theoretical approach for understanding grief and loss, that it seems to be written in tablets of stone for many practitioners. People are then expected somehow to travel from stage to stage, through shock, denial, anger, bargaining, depression and acceptance (Kübler-Ross, 1969). Helpful though these facets undoubtedly are in shaping our understanding of, and sensitivity to, the experience of loss, the reality for many people is far more complex and multi-layered than such a model would suggest. There is no automatic linear progression through the stages, for example, and the concept of acceptance is far more complex than the word might suggest.

One of the exciting aspects of this area of study has been the variety of models which have been put alongside the more traditional explanations. William Worden's notion of the four main tasks of the grieving process, for example, has helped people 'unhook' from the linear, stages approach, and to realise that, in the experience of grief and loss people can be undertaking a range of different emotional tasks at the same time (for a more detailed introduction and critique, see Thompson 2002a, pp. 3ff).

The following discussion of two recent models is not intended to dismiss all other theories and models 'root and branch', but simply to illustrate how a spiritual and religious dimension can flow naturally and easily from them, and that the topics which they raise have a spiritual and religious dimension.

Meaning reconstruction theory is principally associated with the work of Robert Neimeyer (Neimeyer, 2001, for example). Major loss challenges our 'taken-for-granted' world-view, he argues, so much so that:

we are faced with the onerous task of revising these taken-for-granted meanings to be adequate to the changed world we now occupy. Simultaneously we must deal with urgent questions about what this loss signifies, whether something of value might be salvaged from the rubble of the framework which once sheltered us, and who we are now in light of the loss or losses sustained. All of this questioning plays out on levels that are practical, existential and spiritual, and all of it is negotiated using a fund of meanings (partially) shared with others, making it as much a social as a personal process. (2002, p. 48)

To fully understand this model requires a detailed reading of Neimeyer's own work, but even from this cursory introduction several strands become clear. First of all, there is no time limit upon the process of reconstructing a sense of meaning. Some may achieve this quickly; for others it make take years; some may never complete the process. Second, however important other people in our network and cultural group may be, ultimately it is we ourselves who have to make this journey and to find, or make, sense of what has happened and is still happening to us. In this regard the metaphor of a journey may feel very encouraging to many people. A new or revised meaning does not just 'happen': it requires a commitment on our part to help formulate it. Third, the new or revised meaning we discover or create will not seek to draw a curtain inexorably over the past, but will somehow seek to encompass the memories into a present and future framework. Fourth, some losses trigger off an intense need in people to find out about how their loved ones died, especially if this was in the context of a disaster or serious accident. The search for some 'explanations', however impartial, seems to help in the process of moving on and finding meaning for the future. Finally, there seems to be some evidence to suggest that people who are able to look to the future with at least some measure of optimism following a loss will make a better 'fist' of their futures (Franz et al., 2001).

If spirituality may be defined, as it has been in this book, as what we do to give expression to our chosen world-view, then the links with meaning reconstruction theory are clear. Serious loss involves at first a 'checking out' of the world-view which had previously sustained us, and if this is then found to be wanting, a process of revision needs to be undertaken in order to make all the pieces of the jigsaw fit together with a reasonable degree of accuracy.

The religious perspective is particularly important in the area of serious loss precisely because it can put large question marks against people's perceptions of what a Supreme Being has been getting up to. Many people subconsciously at least regard religion as a sort of insurance policy to protect them against 'the slings and arrows of outrageous fortune'. And so, when an arrow strikes, the responses can often be couched in specifically religious terms. For example,

Why did God allow this to happen?

I've led a good God-fearing life, so why should this happen to me?

> Why didn't God heal my partner? He/she was too good to die, especially when you
> see so many evil things happening around us.

Doka (2002) captures this well in his exploration of loss and the 'spiritual assumptive world'. He argues that there are not only individual and specific assumptions we make about the world – for example, that a couple will grow old together – but also the more global assumptions. He writes:

> A loss such as death can cause individuals to challenge many of their global
> assumptions that relate to spirituality. These can entail such issues as the belief in or
> nature of God or a higher power that controls human destiny, a sense of fairness and
> justice in the operation of the world, or belief about what makes life or death
> meaningful. (p. 50)

It is worth noting in passing that the impact can be just as great upon people who previously did not espouse a particular faith system. This is not just to acknowledge the phenomenon of 'death-bed conversions': it also recognises that 'life-changing' events can awaken people to the dimensions of spirituality and at times religion, where previously this had not been significant to them.

Against this background, meaning reconstruction theory may lead people in one of two ways: they will either try to re-think their theology (although that technical word may not be used) so that their understanding of the divine Being becomes more comprehensive; or they will jettison all notions of a divine Being as being intellectually or morally inadequate. Such loss, or rejection, of faith can be a very powerful experience for some people as they face an existential emptiness which hitherto had been unknown. By contrast others may believe, as devout Muslims do for example (although they are not alone in this), that everything that happens is, and indeed *must be*, according to the will of Allah, and that events such as deep loss present a challenge to the believer to submit even more trustingly to the will of Allah (Islam means 'submission to Allah'). The meaning reconstruction in this case is about the process of acknowledging that the human perspective is necessarily flawed and incomplete.

Such examples illustrate something of the sensitivity needed by the human services practitioner, especially if the world-view which they have chosen is at odds with the one which upholds the person with whom they are working. But the meaning reconstruction model opens the door to the opportunity to discuss such issues with people. It may or may not be appropriate for the worker to share their own world-view with the person who is going through the crisis of loss (most of the time it is probably not appropriate), but the main thrust of this book is that part of best practice is to enter into these discussions when appropriate, and to realise the spiritual significance of them.

The second model to explore in this context is Stroebe and Schut's (1999) 'dual process' approach to loss and grief. Again, as with previous models, the application to a wide range of losses is important, even though the model was first presented in a framework of bereavement.

Stated simply, this model suggests that a person experiencing loss begins to live in a world where there are two main 'orientations': a loss orientation and a restoration orientation. Like the two-headed divinity of the new year, Janus, there is a looking to the past, and a looking forward to the future. The crucial aspect of this model is that anyone experiencing a period of severe loss moves in and out of (or 'oscillates' between) these two orientations all the time, often several times in a day or in an hour even. One moment there are floods of tears; the next moment the doorbell rings and a gas meter has to be read, and the matter is handled with appropriate efficiency. One moment there is bleak despair which roots you to the spot with dreadful helplessness; the next moment it is 3 o'clock and you have to fetch the children from school, so you get ready and go out to make sure they are safe. This model suggests that, for as far as the eye can see into our future, we will be moving in and out of these two orientations. As time goes on, we may find ourselves with a greater future focus than we had even dreamed possible; but there will always be those other moments when something triggers a return to the loss-orientation and it comes upon us fresh once more. The key thing is to recognise that our journey 'from here on in' will consist of *both* aspects, and the way we travel on this journey will be unique to us. No one can tell us in which orientation to be in at any time in order to 'do it properly'. It is 'our call', our journey, and we will, by and large, do it *our* way.

Again, this metaphor of the journey offers help and encouragement both to the person experiencing the loss, and to the human services practitioner who may be caught up with them in a helping relationship. Tempting though it may be to tell people how they ought to be feeling, because this or that theory says so, the 'dual process' model puts control back into the hands of the person whose journey it is. The speed at which they travel; the decisions whether to not to pause at certain landmarks, and when (or whether) to go back and re-visit them from time to time, are all in the control of the journey maker, not the professional travelling companion. It is in the journey itself – some who are happy with more religious language might prefer to call it a pilgrimage – that new meaning is discovered. And it is probably only if a person comes to rest and gets profoundly 'stuck' in some way that the professional travelling companion needs to act in order to ensure that some skilled 'roadside maintenance ' is available to enable the journey to get under way once more.

Within this context, the definition of spirituality chosen for the purposes of this book – spirituality being what we do to give expression to our chosen world-view – once again has some important things to say. The metaphor of a journey is a very active one, and how people choose to make that journey – the people they choose to travel with; the destinations they pause or stop at; the organisations they join or withdraw from; the causes they support or from now on choose to neglect – all this gives clues as to their world-view, and the extent to which they find it satisfying, emotionally, intellectually, and indeed spiritually. These metaphorical landmarks – in the territory of both the loss and restoration orientations – can give their professional travelling companion hints and clues as to what is becoming important for the person they are working with, and how they can best respond in a creative, empathetic and creative way.

For those people who belong to faith communities, of course, the journey has some similarities in that every journey is a human one to undertake. In many religions there is a strong sense of the divine Being in some mysterious way accompanying them on their journey, giving them hope and endurance, and a sense of ultimate destination. It is important for the human services practitioner to respect the views of those who belong to such faith communities, but also to be sensitive to those occasions when that person may feel let down by faith colleagues, or perhaps no longer able to trust the belief system shared by others. At such moments the sensitive understanding of a human services practitioner can be extremely important.

So far, the discussion has made links between loss theory and spirituality, and has made the point that although the models being explored have had a primary focus upon bereavement, they can also apply equally helpfully to other experiences of loss. In effect, every human services practitioner, no matter what their areas of practice, can explore the usefulness of these models, and understand the close links to spirituality and at times religion, in the work they are doing with people.

There is one final point that needs to be made, and this concerns perhaps the biggest issue of all – the meaning of death itself. It is likely that for many people the issue of death and our mortality raises in the sharpest way the question of meaning.

It makes you think!

It puts everything else into perspective!

are but two comments that are often heard in the face of sudden death or time of great tragedy. The big WHY? question is asked, implicitly or explicitly, and not just by those most intimately involved. It is a question which philosophers have grappled with, and one about which most, if not all belief systems – religious or non-religious – have something to say. In some profound way, the answers (if that is the right word) which arise from our particular chosen world-view to the question about the meaning and purpose of life ('what is it all about?') are frequently voiced most clearly in the face of death. Here again this is an issue which is shared 'across the board', no matter whether we seek to help people in a professional capacity or are on the receiving end of professional help – or both. Scratch any of us deep enough, and somewhere some sort of answer will emerge. Many believe in some sort of 'afterlife', and this gives them both a sense of hope and purpose for their daily living. Many believe that death is the absolute end, and this too shapes their views about how life should be lived. In the context, therefore, of finding or giving meaning to life, the issue of death places the question in its sharpest focus, and is perhaps the clearest arena where a human services practitioner needs to be aware of, and be able to explore sensitively, issues of religion and spirituality with those whom they are seeking to help.

Chapter 7
Forgiveness

'Forgive me if I have missed the point here, but . . .'

As with many other 'big' words, 'forgiveness' can be used in an almost casual way, as in the example above. It provides an alternative to the lightweight use of the word 'sorry' as we bump into someone in the shopping mall and carry on as if nothing has happened. We offer a mildly apologetic grunt, but nothing more. It certainly does not cost us very much.

By contrast, the heavyweight use of the word, if we may use such a term, is most often associated with religion and faith communities, and with the wayside pulpit posters on display outside church buildings which assault us in traffic jams. Forgiveness is, after all, a religious and theological concept without which most, if not all, faith systems would crumble. It points to the quality of the relationship between the divine Being (however conceived) and individual human 'becomings' whose journey through life is characterised by umpteen failures and shortcomings. Therefore a constant and continued claiming and accepting of divine forgiveness becomes an essential ingredient for anyone belonging to a faith community. With divine help, individuals can be picked up and dusted down, be encouraged to make a fresh start, and have another 'go' at the complexities of human living. The association of the concept of forgiveness with faith communities and religion is therefore quite clear.

However, from the perspective of the human services practitioner and the range of human issues which confront us on a daily basis, no matter what group of people we work with, there is the important question about whether there is any middle ground between these two uses of this important word. Can the concept of 'forgiveness' find a place in their working vocabulary? Does it have any relevance? Can it speak to the large number of people who pass the urgent-sounding, but often faded roadside posters, and pay not a moment's notice to them *precisely because* it is 'God-talk' and they wish to have nothing whatsoever to do with 'that sort of thing'.

As we have noted earlier in the discussion, one of the difficulties in exploring the theme of religion and spirituality is the search for common ground, and in finding ways in which people's experience can be illuminated and enriched by concepts which previously they had dismissed as irrelevant or not part of 'their scene'. If, however, the context can be reshaped, and perhaps become aligned with the concepts of 'change and guilt', then some links may become much more apparent. 'Change' is, after all, at the heart of much human services practice, and the experience of feeling guilty about certain aspects of human behaviour is common to a wider range of people who use these services.

Guilt may be a common enough experience, but it is important to bring some clarity to what is often an ill-defined term. Gordon (2000) suggests that there are three forms of guilt:

(i) Transgression guilt – here the person has actually done something wrong and the feelings of guilt are justifiable and understandable;

(ii) Perfection guilt – comes from falling short of one's own or other people's standards and expectations. In other words, the person fails to achieve idealistic standards;

(iii) Rejection guilt – is the product of serious rejection by significant others. This form of guilt stems from 'serious emotional deprivation and verbal and physical abuse. Because the treatment they received was undeserved, the guilt feelings were false'.

(cited in Swinton, 2001, p. 162)

The first two of these definitions can be linked in with the definition of spirituality being adopted for this book – spirituality is what we do to give expression to our chosen world-view. But before we focus on them, it is worth exploring the third definition in some detail.

Rejection guilt is somewhat different from the first two in that the world-view in these instances has, in a deep sense, been *forced upon* someone by the perpetration of abuse. They have been *made to feel* unclean, dirty, guilty, unworthy and lacking in dignity *as a direct result of the abuse which they have been forced to experience.* In such instances it is the perpetrator who needs to feel the guilt before any change in behaviour can be achieved. From the victim/survivor perspective, their crucial need is to have their self-respect nurtured back, and to be accepted for the valued person they are in their own right. Any sense of their needing forgiveness would be counterproductive; it would suggest that somehow they are to blame for the abuse they have undergone. If anything it would increase the burden forced onto them by the perpetrator.

This is not to say, of course, that the victims/survivors do not experience feelings akin to guilt. Many do. In fact, we know that part of a perpetrator's repertoire is the capacity to make their victims feel that they must take some, perhaps even all, of the blame for the perpetrator's abusive behaviour. The task of the human services practitioner could be seen therefore, in part at least, as being a catalyst in helping to remove the 'sick' world-view which has been forced onto the person who has been abused, and helping them reclaim a world-view where they have dignity and 'specialness' simply by being who they are.

It is important to give full weight to this role which a human services practitioner can fulfil in such situations. It stems from the value base of human dignity, individual worth, self-determination, and the rejection of any abusive behaviour.

This value base underpins social work and social care, health care, youth work and advice work; and although the extent to which these issues may be discussed with a victim/survivor may vary according to the agency involved, the fundamental principle remains. The spiritual dimension of this, of course, takes us to the very heart of what we believe it means to be human, how we should treat each other, and our responsibility to challenge oppressive abusive behaviour when we encounter it.

The second definition of guilt has a clear resonance with a person's chosen world-view, although here again the extent to which the world-view is consciously chosen *by* them, or *for* them by their parents' or by other significant people's treatment of them in their early years, is an important question to bear in mind. Nevertheless, the issue is clear: there are people who set themselves unrealistically high achievement targets, and work to such a stringently perfectionist agenda that they can only fall short. That is the point: as with the myth of Sisyphus who would never be able to reach the summit with his rock-pushing task, so too perfectionists can never quite reach their pinnacles of achievement. For some, of course, this scenario remains a creative challenge which helps them bring the best out of themselves; but for others a sense of guilt for under-achievement can soon take over. Indeed the question is not whether they will fall short – that is guaranteed – but rather the extent to which they will develop a sense of failure, and how heavy will be the subsequent burden of guilt they have imposed upon themselves. The world-view which underpins such behaviour has something to do with how such 'driven' people value themselves. They measure their self-worth against a benchmark of an ultimately unattainable achievement, and feel guilty as a result.

Here again the role of the human services practitioner will vary according to the profession. There may, or may not be a need for psychological intervention to help the thwarted guilt-ridden perfectionist reshape their world-view. But they will need somehow to learn how to be easier on themselves, and to begin to realise their intrinsic worth, rather than being controlled by a culture where self-worth has somehow to be earned or deserved. The crucial point for the human services practitioner to take seriously is that the suggestion or offer of forgiveness from a third party in such a scenario would only serve to reinforce the very system which is creating the guilt in the first place: 'Come on Sisyphus – next time try just that bit harder and I am sure you will make it to the top'. The implication is that the task *is* achievable and if, for any reason, there is failure, it is the fault of the person, not the impossible nature of the task.

Paradoxically, the person at the centre of it all will still need to find a way forward to accepting and even forgiving themselves before any sense of healing or completeness can be achieved. But forgiveness in this sense is less about acknowledging wrongdoing, or an unwillingness to give it 100 per cent effort, and much more about recognising the need for a somewhat reconfigured world-view.

Such a change would help the person centre stage to be much more gentle with themselves and to celebrate their intrinsic value and worth, irrespective of their accomplishments. They could begin to measure themselves by what they have been able to achieve, rather than by what is ultimately impossible to attain.

The first definition of guilt is perhaps more familiar to everyone, and is much more likely to feature somewhere in the workloads of most human services practitioners. In the widest sense, we are all conscious of the times when we make a mess of things; when we 'get hold of the wrong end of the stick' and upset people unnecessarily; when we find ourselves behaving in ways which cause pain to other people; when we are so caught up with our own 'agendas' that we ignore the legitimate needs of others. When the impact of our behaviour begins to dawn on us, and the repercussions of our actions become clear, it is likely that most people will feel anything from a slight twinge to a powerful attack of guilty feelings. We know then that we have done something wrong. It is what happens next that brings us into the realm of spirituality, and the actions we take as a result of the world-view we hold.

Although there are undoubtedly some people whose life skills seem to be particularly focused on trampling on the lives of other people with a psychopathic disregard for their feelings or ultimate value, for many others the realisation of wrongdoing more often engenders a sense of guilt and a question about how things can be put right. The issue of change, in other words, is firmly on the agenda. Their world-view is not comfortable with the amount of hurt or upset which they have caused, and so they feel instinctively that they need to do something to put things right. And one of the crucial steps in this process – perhaps even, the first step – is this issue of forgiveness.

Canda and Furman (1999) note that:

> Forgiveness of self or others can be an important step in releasing pain and preoccupation with feelings of guilt, shame or anger towards oneself and anger and hostility towards others (Garvin 1998). Therapeutic forgiveness does not mean 'forgive and forget', because it is often impossible and undesirable to forget an injustice or an outrage. We need to learn from our mistakes and also to move on. We need to take proactive stands against indignity and injustice against ourselves and others, but without being stuck in an adversarial mentality and way of life. Indeed, forgiveness can open up energy and insight for more effective action. 'Forgiveness is conceptually defined as letting go of the need for vengeance and releasing associated negative feelings such as bitterness and resentment' (DiBlasio p. 163). (p. 304)

All this suggests that words are not enough, although they are often an important starting point. It is what we do to channel our sorrow at hurting others, into some actions which will begin to put things right, that really matters.

Examples from the wide range of work undertaken by human services practitioners easily come to mind. Relationships which begin to falter; children and young people whose behaviour brings them into conflict with parental or authority figures; neighbours in dispute; abusive and exploitative behaviour towards children, young people, adults and elders; harassment on the basis of gender, sexuality, disability: the list is endless. And the one thing which they all have in common is that such behaviours need to be challenged and changed, because they contravene our values and beliefs and world-views about how people should be treated and respected.

The process of working with people to effect change is a mainstream activity for many human services practitioners. Social workers, probation officers and prison officers come most readily to mind, but youth workers, psychologists and advice workers also fulfil this role from time to time. The role which forgiveness can play in this process is of great importance, and is being increasingly recognised in secular settings as well as in specifically religious contexts.

Several strands can be identified. First, an important step in the process of effecting change is for people to be able to forgive themselves for the occasions on which they have let themselves down by acting in such negative and damaging ways. This has resonances with the recovery regime advocated for those who misuse drugs or alcohol and wish either to reduce their involvement with these substances, or to become 'clean'. The first step in the process is not only to admit that the problem exists, but also to acknowledge that people owe it to themselves to accept that the process of change is worthwhile. As long as they do not think that they are worthy of living a better, more fulfilled life, then change will not happen.

A second stage, which is becoming increasingly recognised in the criminal justice system for example, is the determination to do something to demonstrate that the sorrow or remorse for the negative or antisocial behaviour is really meant. Reparation schemes, and opportunities for offenders to meet with their victims to hear about the impact of their offending behaviour, are becoming increasingly popular. When faced with the full consequences of their actions, people may be more likely to put into effect those changes in lifestyle which are necessary to reduce the level of suffering inflicted upon others.

A third stage is perhaps the most significant, when people who have inflicted hurt upon others openly apologise for their actions and ask for the other person's forgiveness. There is nothing automatic in this process: it will 'cost' a lot for the person who is asking for forgiveness, and it will 'cost' the person who has been injured in whatever way, to agree to forgive the person who has hurt them. But if the forgiveness is genuinely requested and willingly granted, then the restoration of the relationship can be at a far deeper and more honest level than before.

From the victim/survivor's perspective, however, the hurt may run so deep that such hope for a reconciliation is neither possible nor appropriate. But this is not to say that in such cases forgiveness is a 'non-starter'. On the contrary, there is likely to come a point where the anger, bitterness and resentment is eating so deeply into their lives that the original hurt is being exacerbated, and the quality of the person's life is even more diminished. In these situations, if the victim/survivor can find a mechanism for letting go of the resentment – be this through a personal act of affirmation, or through a counselling or a religiously based intervention if this is appropriate – then there is a chance that a new future can open up as a result of this act of forgiveness.

The issue of forgiveness was highlighted by The Forgiveness Project (1993) whose work was spotlighted in an exhibition in London by OMD Snapshots. It featured the results from a small-scale research project conducted with 906 adults in December 2003 in London, which showed that 55 per cent thought that forgiveness is an essential part of the healing process, and 14 per cent believed that, if someone has been forgiven for their crime, it should be reflected in their punishment. Three quotations linked to this exhibition are worth including at this point. Graham Waddington, from the Thames Valley Police, observed that:

> Currently, the criminal justice system makes no allowances for apology, which is all that many victims of crime are looking for. This alienates both victims and perpetrators. It is refreshing to see some public recognition of the vital role of forgiveness in the criminal justice system.

Lucie Russell, Director of Smart Justice, commented that:

> This is a fascinating survey which highlights the fact that forgiveness could be an essential part of the healing process within criminal justice. Restorative Justice schemes where offenders meet their victims not only help the victim to move forward, but because offenders have to face up to the impact of their crime has caused, have had dramatic results in reducing re-offending, thus creating safer communities.

A further powerful comment came from Tim Newell, former Governor of Grendon Underwood Prison, who said that:

> It's interesting to see that people recognise how essential forgiveness is to recovery. The main dynamic which stops victims, offenders and their communities of care from moving on after the trauma of a crime is the inability to forgive the person responsible for the crime. This identifies forever the person with the deed and can freeze relationships and life stories for ever.

This section began with the question whether some middle ground could be discovered between a casual use of 'forgive' and its 'heavy-duty' religious connotations, in which human services practitioners could feel 'at home' in the range of work they undertake. The discussion has explored various aspects of guilt, change and forgiveness to demonstrate that such ground does indeed exist. The language used has deliberately avoided any religious or spiritual overtones, although any reader who belongs to a faith community will have quickly made links to those dimensions. But in the context of the definition of spirituality adopted for this book, there are some important points that deserve to be drawn out.

1. Any acknowledgment of guilt or remorse has a spiritual dimension in that it puts us in touch with our understanding of the sort of people we are or could be. It reminds us of our vulnerability, our capacity to inflict harm as well as to do good, and the feelings which this generates within us.
2. It points up the world-view which we hold, and challenges us to locate our behaviour within a framework which has the capacity to offer some sort of rationale which can encompass our negative actions, as well as the potential for putting things right. Some faith systems are particularly strong in this area, but such frameworks are by no means limited to religious systems.
3. Forgiveness as an activity has a strong value base which respects other people as being intrinsically worthy as individuals. Here again there are strong links with faith systems in this regard.
4. Forgiveness does not carry with it any implication that abuse is anything other than abuse. Any activity which damages other people or severely limits their life chances or quality of life is to be roundly condemned, and if necessary subject to the full weight of the law and its penalties. Forgiveness is not 'going soft', but is the opportunity for a courageous new start.
5. There is nothing automatic about forgiveness. It is costly to request and costly to grant, but if it has a full impact upon all those involved it can transform relationships.
6. As with any major event which has an impact upon our lives, our world-view needs either to be capable of incorporating such new dimensions, or to be open to challenge, or even to replacement by a more satisfying world-view.

One final point needs to be made. So far the emphasis of the discussion has been upon individual behaviour, by and large, and this is without doubt a huge important dimension. But it has wider connotations, as Professor Marc Ellis, the distinguished Jewish theologian, who has been challenging his own people's abuse of the Palestinians, makes clear. He writes that:

> forgiveness could only come within a commitment to justice. 'People cannot simply "forgive" – invite back into their lives on a mutual basis – those who continue to violate us', one student wrote, 'otherwise "forgiveness" is an empty word. Forgiveness is possible only when the violence stops. Only then can those who have been violated even consider the possibility of actually loving those who once brutalised and battered them. Only then can the former victims empower the victimisers by helping them to realise their own power to live as liberated liberators, people able to see in themselves and others a corporate capacity to shape the future'. It is in the ending of injustice and the journey towards a mutual and just future that forgiveness becomes revolutionary. (Ellis, 2000, p. 276)

Here a new corporate dimension enters the discussion, and it provides an important link to the third main theme of this section: social justice.

Chapter 8
Social Justice

There is no doubt that the themes of religion and spirituality are seen by many as being intensely personal, private even. They touch our lives at the deepest level, and illuminate what some call the 'core of our being'. They are issues which may be deeply held and intensely felt, but are not shared or discussed with others very often. From the human services practitioner's point of view, it may be important to uncover such issues in an attempt to understand how the person who has come for help really 'ticks', but it all still remains at the individual level.

The definition of spirituality adopted for this book, however – spirituality being what we do to give expression to our chosen world-view – will not allow it to stop there. Certainly there is a strong individualistic strand to the definition, but it also has an important societal dimension. Our world-views will clearly need to be intellectually and emotionally satisfying to us individually, by giving us some insight into our place within the wider fabric of society, and also (for those within certain faith communities) a hope for our ultimate destiny. But a wider understanding of spirituality is called for if this definition is to hold.

I have explored this dimension in a previous work when I argued that:

> One final dimension needs to be raised, a dimension which has common threads in both faith-community and more general definitions of spirituality. This is the dimension of passion and justice. Alongside very personal and private views of spirituality there are wider perspectives which find expression certainly in the monotheistic traditions. Here we find that a real love of the divine being (however conceived) and a real commitment to what is required of people of faith, is measured not by the fulsomeness of piety, but by the degree of zeal for truth and justice, in seeing right prevail, captives set free, and the hungry fed. (Moss, 2002, p. 38)

Here we have an important dimension to this discussion which will perhaps echo the concerns expressed in much contemporary human service practice which seeks to challenge discrimination and oppression. It is not enough to apply the sticking plaster and bandages on individual wounds if the problems which are causing the pain are more deep-seated and societal in nature. Of course, it is essential that individuals receive the care they need and deserve, but if the fundamental causes are not addressed, then the queue for help will simply get longer and longer.

This dimension to religion and spirituality, however, is not widely recognised. And yet the world-views which are offered by various faith systems do have a component which takes seriously these issues of social justice, because they are intrinsically bound up with the world-view they espouse. It is worth pausing now, therefore, to give some examples which illustrate this point, albeit very briefly.

Judaism

The story of the Jewish faith is a complex one, with a powerful 'leitmotif' of suffering at the hands of the oppressor. Early experiences of exile, and the suffering which was etched upon the nation's soul as a result, remains a dominant strand which has only been strengthened by events such as the Holocaust. Alongside these experiences has been the conviction that they have been a chosen people, and that however great the desolation, their God (Adonay*) will not only rescue and liberate them, but will ultimately vindicate them in the eyes of the world as the channel through which the goodness of Yahweh will stream for the benefit of all (see for example Isaiah 60 vv 1–3 in the Hebrew bible). Fundamental to their life has been the Torah: and its commentaries and interpretations in the Talmud which offer both general and at times very detailed guidance as to how people should live one with another. In this sense, it is a religion of the book, where the obligations towards family and community are spelled out. The covenant relationship between Adonay and the chosen people needs to be reflected in the ways in which people treat each other with justice (zsedakah lit. righteousness), loyal devotion (hesed lit. kindness), and peace (shalom).

In other words, the world-view of being a people called into being and chosen by Adonay, lays obligations upon its members: an inward-looking self-centredness is simply not part of the package, however pious or spiritual the person may be. (Deuteronomy 7 vv 7–8; 9: 4–7)

Alongside this is an important strand where oppressive and discriminatory practices are identified and challenged. This is seen in people called prophets, who acted as the conscience of the nation by reminding them of the full implications of the world-view which they shared. Thus we find Amos challenging the Jewish people with these words:

> You have oppressed the poor and robbed them of their grain . . . you persecute good people, take bribes and prevent the poor from getting justice in the courts. Make it your aim to do what is right, not what is evil, so that you may live. Then the lord God Almighty really will be with you as you claim he[sic] is. Hate what is evil, love what is right and see that justice prevails in the courts . . . let justice flow like a stream, and righteousness like a river that never runs dry. (Amos 5 vv 11–24 selected verses. See also Isaiah 35 vv 1–10 and 61 vv 1–4; Micah 6 vv 6–8 in the Hebrew Bible)

---

* The Hebrew letters used in their sacred writings for Being Divine, YHWH – known as the tetragrammation – were never spoken. Jews believe the Divine Name is so special that it should never be spoken. They therefore substitute Adonay or Adonai instead, meaning 'Behold'. For this reason Adonay will be used throughout this book.

Although some would argue that 'by and large the framework of justice seems to be legalistic and retributive' (Thakur, 1996, p. 35, for example), the significance of the prophetic strand should not be underestimated for the impact it has had within both Christianity and Islam, and also in more secular manifestations and commitments to social justice. Within Judaism there is also the strong future messianic hope that one day peace between all peoples will reign for ever.

Here we find a passion for justice; a sense of outrage that some people were being treated unfairly; a deep yearning for liberation, all located within a world-view which was saying something about how these deep concerns stemmed from an understanding of the nature of the supreme being to whom the Jewish people believed they owed their very existence.

Some more detail has been given in this section than in some of the following ones because some of the themes find echoes in later faith systems.

Islam

Much of Islam as a faith system acknowledges the debt it owes to both Judaism and Christianity, and respects their moral teachings and writings. Righteousness and justice are upheld as core values, and stem from an obedience and submission to Allah. As in Judaism, so too with Islam there is a central corpus of influential writings, principally the Qur'an (the revealed word of Allah in Arabic given to the prophet Mohammed (p.b.u.h. = peace be upon him) whose example is contained in the Sharia, 'the way' or the law).

Some key injunctions to lead a holy and upright life, where justice is at the centre, are expressed in Chapter 2 v 110; 148; 177; 215, and in Chapter 4 v 135 which says:

> Establish justice (al-qist) being witnesses for God – even if the evidence goes against yourselves or against your parents and kinsmen; and irrespective of whether the witness is rich or poor; under all circumstances God has priority. (cited in Thakur, 1996, p. 39)

Alongside this are the injunctions to give to charity and to cultivate a generous disposition towards others. There is also within some aspects of Islam the future hope that injustice, oppression and tyranny will be swept away by Allah, and a true harmony established for all who live in obedience to the will of Allah.

Again the world-view is important. Muslims believe that issues of human justice are of concern to them precisely because it is a concern of Allah, and that the essential obedience to Allah which is at the heart of the faith brings with it a concern for social justice.

Hinduism

Although a different kind of faith system from the monotheism of Judaism and Islam (and also Christianity), Hinduism has a strong sense of cosmic order which is to be reflected in those who subscribe to its world-view. This is based on Rig Veda, one of the four main sacred writings of Hinduism (the Vedas). Here there is an emphasis upon the idea of 'dharma' which stands for the 'cosmic order, the law, justice, morality and the very fabric of social order' (Thakur, p. 29). Within Hinduism there is the notion that the deeds in this life will influence the quality and type of living experienced in the next life, for good or ill (karma). This provides a strong encouragement for people to live a life where the needs of others are taken into account. There is also the hope for a golden age of justice, peace and plenty, although unlike other faith systems this golden age will not necessarily be at the end: it too may crumble and fade away in the endless cycle. There is nevertheless a strong emphasis upon the virtues of justice and right dealing between people, enshrined most famously in the life and work of Mahatma Gandhi and his tireless work for the non-violent liberation of his people.

Atheism and humanism

It is important to recognise that for many people there is as deep a spirituality within the bundle of beliefs which constitute an atheistic/humanist world-view as in any of the faith systems to which others subscribe. It is probably less appropriate to talk of doctrines in this context, as that term has religious connotations which many atheists and humanists would clearly reject. Nevertheless many of the contributions to art, music and culture, as well as politics, are made by people who have no religious affiliations, but who nevertheless would acknowledge and own a spiritual dimension to their lives, in the way in which they view and value the natural world and their responsibilities to other human beings. Whether they work through organised politics or through pressure groups or interest groups, there is a clear commitment to social justice and the improvement of the quality of life for others. Unlike faith communities, there is a less identifiable 'clubbable quality' among atheists or humanists, partly because their chosen world-view does not require it in the same way as a religious faith system would, and partly because there are not so many common denominators as in an organisation which people consciously choose to join. This is not to say of course that everyone who espouses this world-view would believe the same things or engage in similar activities – far from it – but for the purposes of this book it is important to recognise that the passion for justice which is an important dimension to spirituality has taken root in the lives of many people who have no religious allegiance, but whose commitment to the betterment of the social order burns as fiercely and as brightly as anyone else's.

Christianity

Many of the points already made in connection with Judaism and Islam hold true for Christianity, which was born in the same middle Eastern cradle. It shares with

Judaism some of the same passion for justice and obedience to the will of God. It shares with Islam the significant influence of its founder, although the claims for the person of Christ far exceed those made in later generations for Mohammed. Christ's teachings around the theme of social justice are based on the notions of loving one's neighbour, refusing to take revenge, and being willing to forgive without limit. A further dimension to Christ's teachings is on the idea of the Kingdom of God. These are couched in such everyday language that it is reasonable to imply that they were standards which he felt people could not only aspire to but also attain in their relationships one with the other.

A prophetic strand in the teaching also challenged the religious authorities of the day for their neglect of justice. Parables such as the Good Samaritan (Luke 10 vv 25–37) and the great judgment between the sheep and the goats (Matthew 25 vv 31–46) have immense power precisely because the acid test of faithfulness was whether people cared for the wounded, fed the hungry, clothed the poor and visited the sick (see too Luke 1 vv 46–55 which still reads like a political manifesto of what the world could look like).

Once more the same point needs to be made: the world-view which claims that everything owes its existence to the creative power of God makes demands of its followers to mirror in their own lives the living and forgiving nature of God which they have been invited to enjoy through Christ.

These snapshots (and they are nothing more than that) into a number of world-views have illustrated the central theme of this section. Religion and spirituality are to be seen in a context much wider than individual and self-centred interest. There is within many of these world-views, religious and secular, a burning passion for justice and the improvement of living conditions for the people who inhabit this planet. As Brandon (2000) notes: 'The spiritual road is about living out our *uniqueness*, not our individualism' (p. 17).

This concern for justice can be summarised as follows:

> In this passionate conviction that all deserve equality of treatment and respect, there is an underlying passionate spirituality that has an energy and a restlessness that will not find peace until truth and justice prevail. Maybe if more of this spirituality had been in evidence in recent decades, some of the antipathy between social work, as just one of the human services for example, and spirituality might have been avoided. (Moss, 2002, p. 38)

This review of some of the more political and social justice dimensions to spirituality has tried to make clear the strong links which could exist between human services practitioners and the great themes of religion and spirituality. However much human services practitioners are caught up in the everyday needs of individuals who come to them for help, advice or treatment, there is always the wider dimension that underpins their work. Anti-discriminatory, anti-oppressive, emancipatory practice – to use some buzz words which are familiar in social work and social care, but have wider implications for all human services practitioners – are all pointers to wider issues of social justice. It is not good enough to assume that all problems are the fault of the individual, and to seek to pathologise each and every condition which we encounter. There are some wider forces at work which we need to take into account.

Interestingly, and somewhat as an aside, there are some further links with some of the religious world-views on these wider issues. We have become familiar with the experience of oppression and discrimination as powerful forces in society which have a serious and at times debilitating impact upon the lives of individual people. We know about the range of 'isms' which operate in a similar way: racism, sexism, classism, disablism and so on. There are some clear parallels with what, in the Christian world-view for example, are called by St Paul the 'principalities and powers and rules of this dark age' (Ephesians 6 v 12). We do not have to 'buy into' his personalising of the forces of evil to appreciate that Paul was clearly aware that there are some powerful forces (or 'isms') at work in society which have to be challenged and eradicated if people are to have the life chances they deserve.

As examples of this we can reflect on the experience of the wide range of human services practitioners being included in this book, to explore some of the practice implications arising from this discussion about social justice.

Practice implications

- *Advice workers* spend a huge amount of time with individuals who are overwhelmed by mountains of debt, or who are not receiving the benefits to which they are entitled. Organisations such as Citizens' Advice, therefore, have a social policy dimension to their work. This seeks deliberately to understand some of the wider issues which are affecting the life-chances of people in their communities, so that they can put pressure on Government at local and national level to make appropriate changes to the system.
- *Youth and community workers* spend a lot of time working with young people who sometimes have to live with the stigmatising label 'disaffected'. Excluded often from education, their life chances seem to be dwindling. Workers will spend a lot of time trying to open doors for young people, and to motivate them to find satisfying jobs and careers. But unless something structural is done to recognise and address some of the issues which are causing the 'disaffection', the difficulties will remain.
- *Social workers, probation officers and prison officers* spend a lot of time with a wide range of people who use their services, across all ages and conditions, and frequently encounter ways in which the odds are stacked against certain groups in society. For example older people; people with mental health problems; disabled people; black and Asian people; gay and

lesbian people. Many of these groups still do not feel they are living in a society where equality of opportunity is possible. Although in some ways these human services practitioners, as employees, have limited opportunity for challenging the status quo, the importance of using various channels to highlight major societal concerns cannot be underestimated.

- *Health care workers* spend a lot of time with individual issues of health care, but have a much stronger record than others for initiating research into both community health and individual conditions in order to improve the life-chances of those who come to them for help and treatment.

In all these examples, there is an underlying passion for, and commitment to, social justice by seeking to point up the oppressive discriminatory issues which limit individual life-chances, and to conduct research in order to find ways of enhancing the quality of life for individuals and society as a whole. Here surely a secular spirituality is at work.

In this section there have been several mentions of oppression and discrimination, and in the third part of the book we must now turn to the wide area of anti-discriminatory practice in the context of religion and spirituality.

Part Three: Discrimination and Oppression: Towards a Practice Perspective

Chapter 9
Celebrating Diversity: Setting the Scene

The demands of best practice, as understood by the variety of professional human service practitioners for whom this book has been written, are often enshrined in codes of practice which set out how workers should behave, and what standard of service those who come to them for help should reasonably expect to receive. Underlying such codes of conduct, however, are the core values which the profession or organisation holds, and which it seeks to inculcate in all those who have a role to play within it.

One of the core values which underpins this book is anti-discriminatory practice, a theme which has been widely explored in the literature (see, for example, Thompson, 2001; 2002b, for good introductions to this topic). This theme acknowledges that society is structured in such a way that certain members – black people, disabled people, gay and lesbian people for example – do not get a 'fair crack of the whip'. They are discriminated against in all manner of ways, and it is the responsibility of the human services practitioner to understand that, and to work in such a way as to counteract, wherever possible, the impact of that discrimination upon the person coming to them for help.

In this somewhat complex area, some other allied values also operate: anti-oppressive practice, for example. Some would suggest (for example, Phillipson, 1992) that a distinction needs to be made between anti-discriminatory and anti-oppressive practice, arguing that the former deals with narrow legalistic issues, whilst the latter seeks to deal with more deep-seated issues about how oppression works in society (see also Dalrymple and Burke, 1995, for a discussion on these issues). Thompson (2002b), however, argues strongly against such an approach, and suggests that what some suggest are two approaches should be seen as two sides of the same coin:

> Whether attempts are made to stop the discrimination that leads to oppression, or to deal with the resulting oppression, the primary objective in practice remains broadly the same . . . The starting point is the recognition of diversity as an asset, a positive advantage rather than a problem, and difference, equally, as something that can bestow benefits. (p. 44)

For Thompson it is crucially important to recognise the personal, cultural and structural aspects of anti-discriminatory practice, often referred to as PCS analysis, rather than viewing it in a narrow legalistic sense:

> any approaches to the questions of discrimination and oppression which do not take account of all three of these levels, and their inter-relationships, is in danger of simplifying a very complex set of issues. (pp. 44–5)

What we are dealing with here takes us immediately into the earlier discussion about world-views and the ways in which people's behaviour is affected by the way they view the world. Difference and diversity can be either celebrated or attacked, and it is important to be clear about the value base we use in order to assess which approach is appropriate. Abusive behaviours, for example, are certainly 'different and diverse', and characterise the way in which some people view the world. But the value base held by human services practitioners, which stresses the unique value of each person and their right to be respected and treated with dignity, challenges any world-view which suggests that anyone can be treated otherwise.

The attempt by human services practitioners to operationalise these values can be seen sometimes as something of a 'rescue attempt' in that they will often seek at least to soften or ameliorate the impact of these negative forces and influences on the lives of the people with whom they are working. Women-centred practice, for example, often helps women to focus on the ways in which a patriarchal system has kept them in a secondary, subservient role. That realisation, linked with some achievable strategic objectives, often helps women to take back control of their lives, and to be set free from the discriminatory and oppressive behaviour of others. It has also led to serious challenging of cultural and structural issues which have played a part in this sexist oppression.

For this reason there has been an increasing focus upon emancipatory practice in recent years, with its emphasis upon helping people to be 'set free from' some of the forces and influences which were having a negative impact upon their lives (see Thompson, 2003, for an introduction to this theme).

Thompson argues that:

> whether we tackle the processes that lead to oppression (= anti-discriminatory practice), or deal with the oppression itself (anti-oppressive practice) the overall aim is emancipation from discriminatory and oppressive practices, assumptions, structures, language etc.' (personal correspondence)

The strength of these approaches is that they take seriously at a personal, cultural and societal level the very real negative forces which are at work within society and which diminish the life-chances and opportunities of so many people. Until society can do something to change its shape, it will be important for human services practitioners to address such issues as best they can, within their admitted limitations. It is at this point, however, that the full richness of anti-discriminatory practice needs to be acknowledged: to be seen, in effect, not just as a strategy for tackling problems, serious though they are, but also as a pointer towards a true celebration of diversity.

'Celebrating diversity' has therefore become a sort of benchmark in contemporary human services, which seeks to establish a positive value-statement to underpin best practice. This suggests that the best starting point is for workers to be able to celebrate the very real differences which people bring to a complex society, and to make a point of celebrating the diversity and the enrichment which this brings. This position will fight hard against discrimination and oppression, within a framework which clearly states that society will be the poorer if all parts of the community do not celebrate their full potential. Society will lack the colour and brightness, the vigour and talent which often lies untapped if there is not a positive statement about celebrating diversity at its very heart.

To move to such a position requires a commitment by the traditional majority groups to begin to see things differently. For too long the married, heterosexual white male, with a job, a mortgage and 2.4 children, two cars and a set of brown, green or black wheelie bins – oh yes, and of course a wife who may well wish to go out to work – has been seen as the societal norm. But times have changed, and society can now be infinitely enriched by different styles of family and lifestyle, racial and cultural tradition and various expressions of the work/leisure balance, not to mention the increasing diversity and richness of experience in the 'silver power' of older people in the community. (The more usual 'grey power' epithet seems to lack the sparkle, warmth and zest of what many older people in their 'silver years' can often bring to society.)

The move towards celebrating diversity consciously recognises and values the many types of contribution which can enrich a community, and positively laments the negative impact upon the whole community when certain groups are prevented, for whatever reason, from making their contribution to the tapestry of its life together.

The significance of this for religion and spirituality is clear. The phrase 'emancipatory practice', for example, is one which is likely to ring bells within at least some faith communities. Both Christian and Jewish traditions, for example, share a common history of a people being 'set free' from tyrannical oppression and slavery. One aspect of their theological framework is of a divine Being who sets people free, and this is a theme which has had an enormous appeal to oppressed peoples who yearn for liberation and emancipation, as well as experiencing an inner freedom as individuals. There are close parallels between the PCS analysis discussed by Thompson, and some of these theological insights which also challenge ways in which people can be discriminated against and oppressed at a structural level.

All of this, however, seems at times to be in marked contrast to the individualistic conceptualisation and definition of spirituality which was discussed in Part One, and which has probably served to alienate many human services practitioners who cannot see the links between spirituality and the struggle for social justice and emancipatory practice. Some of this has been captured by Henery (2003) in his review of contemporary theories of spirituality in social work, although his observations have relevance to a wider group of helping professions. He draws attention to the 'spirituality-religion binary', and comments that:

> Spirituality is fluid and developing. Spirituality is about the real me and about my right to find out who I am – to test and taste for myself. Religion, by contrast, is composed of rules, customs and beliefs. Religion is fixed and static. Indeed, religion threatens spirituality as blind authority and dead tradition always threatens to quash the individual. (p. 1110)

The difficulty with this approach, although it undoubtedly highlights the negative impact of religious systems upon individuals, is that it ignores several key issues which human services practitioners need to take into account in their practice. First, it ignores the increasing volume of community-based work undertaken by a range of faith-based organisations to tackle social injustice issues at individual and structural levels. Second, it ignores the reality for many members of faith-based organisations, whose spirituality is somehow expressed in and through their religious affiliation, in spite of the negative institutional influences. The sense of the holy, for example, is sometimes (though by no means exclusively) 'transmitted' through their experience of liturgy and communal worship. Third, for many groups in society their membership of a faith-based organisation affirms and strengthens their social as well as their individual identity and value.

Henery does highlight, however, an important feature at this point, by noting the ways in which minority ethnic groups are:

> Generally characterized as first religious and only then as spiritual. They are, therefore, placed en masse in the disfavoured half of the spirituality-religion binary. (p. 1112)

This may be an example of a subtle racism which not only seeks to deny the richness of spirituality to such groups, but also imposes upon them a set of assumptions and value judgements about religion and religious observance which are not justified. Indeed the whole notion of this 'binary' being the whole story is another example of the ways in which people who belong to faith communities are often marginalised and ignored by many, including some human services practitioners.

If, however, spirituality is understood in a much broader sense which allows – demands even – both cultural and societal dimensions to be included, then the picture changes radically:

Within this framework, the loss of the spiritual is to be deeply mourned, and its gradual recovery something to be celebrated, precisely because of this deep-seated imperative to work at every level for the wholeness and liberation of human beings from everything which enslaves and impoverishes the human spirit. In this sense there will be a powerful clash not between spirituality and those who are arguing passionately for, and striving ceaselessly for emancipatory practice, but rather *between these two new allies on one side* and on the other side the forces of organised religion which . . . have served at times to enslave and diminish and to control. Spirituality becomes . . . the very heart of the struggle for justice and emancipation. (Moss 2002, pp. 43–44, emphasis added)

Perhaps the time has come to explore a further development in PCS analysis by suggesting a further perspective to add to it: spiritual. PCSS would then encompass some of the crucial issues being raised in this book. Not only would the spiritual perspective enrich the other dimensions, but crucially, the other dimensions (P, C and S) would ensure that the spiritual was firmly located within the wider framework which Thompson and others have argued is essential for a relevant best practice for contemporary human services. And if sensitively evaluated, the role of faith-based organisations and the contribution which they can make to individual and community well-being could be creatively subsumed under the heading of spirituality instead of being regarded only in a negative light.

That this remains a challenge for many helping professions is clear. With the notable exception of healthcare and medical professionals who at least have emphasised the contribution which religion and spirituality can play at an individual level, other helping professions have studiously avoided any acknowledgment of the contribution which religion and spirituality can make to individual, let alone community well-being and enrichment. The vast resources of a variety of faith-based organisations being made available to the community for pastoral care, for example, have been regularly overlooked by social workers seeking to put together packages of care in the community.

A further example comes from the field of child protection, fostering and adoption and work with children and families. In a private communication to the author, one concerned professional wrote:

In our organisation we had some input into the Climbié inquiry and have been making a special effort to build stronger links with black majority churches. There is a major job of work to be done, in my opinion, in building bridges between faith communities and the social work establishments. I recently had some discussion with a caller to our help-line who wanted to have her baby adopted by a Christian family and had been told that the local authority didn't set much store in the matching process by religious considerations. They regarded ethnicity as being much more important. (2003)

Perhaps part of the reason for this lies in the suspicion of religious and faith-based organisations already discussed in Part One. There is no doubt that in some areas, the values of some faith-based organisations are clearly at odds with the celebration of diversity which characterises human services practitioners. But a blanket refusal to see the other side of the coin suggests that there are some entrenched positions in urgent need of challenge.

This practice-based discussion has focused on the value base of anti-discriminatory practice, with its further dimensions of anti-oppressive and emancipatory practice, set within a framework of celebrating diversity. The close links between these conceptual frameworks and an understanding of spirituality which includes a passion for justice and emancipation, has also been emphasised. In order to develop a practice perspective, however, which includes spiritual and religious dimensions, it is important to explore a further set of practice-based issues which have important contributions to make. These may be clustered under the heading of strength, power and resilience, and will be addressed in the next chapter.

Chapter 10
Strength, Resilience and Power

Introducing a 'strengths perspective'

Considerable emphasis has been placed in this book upon the importance and impact of the world-views which people hold. The working definition of spirituality which has been adopted suggests that spirituality is what we do to give expression to our chosen world-view. If we see the world in a certain way, then it follows that we will seek to behave in ways which express that world-view. This definition carries with it, of course, the possibility of both negative and positive outcomes. Just as religion has at times been experienced as a negative force in people's lives, so too with spirituality. If a person's world-view is based upon a paradigm of abuse, and leads to abusive behaviour, then that has to be challenged, and vulnerable people have to be protected. The underpinning value base of respect, dignity and worth of each individual provides a litmus test for people's spirituality just as much as any other human activity. If someone's spirituality does not in some sense, directly or indirectly, contribute to the enrichment of humanity, then it stands condemned, or at very least 'sidelined' as narcissistic self-indulgence.

How human services practitioners view the people with whom they are required to work is of fundamental importance, not least because it will influence the way in which they treat them. The advice worker who regards asylum seekers as potential scroungers is likely to find it difficult to accord to them the dignity and respect which is their right as human beings. Nurses who have strong anti-abortion views are likely to find it difficult to treat with care and respect a young woman who comes to them for a second or third termination. Youth workers who regard 'disaffected' young people as lazy and work-shy are going to find it difficult to show them respect and to work with them creatively. Social workers who view older people as helpless and unable to cope are unlikely to see them as resourceful people who may not necessarily need to be 'shunted off' to a home where everything is done for them. Probation officers and prison staff who have themselves been burgled or had their car stolen may find their professionalism challenged when working with people who have committed such offences.

The examples are endless, but the point is clear. Our values affect our behaviour, and how we view the world and other people is of fundamental importance to the sort of people we are and how we treat others.

There is one area of particular importance which deserves attention, which arises directly from the world-view we have as human services practitioners. This concerns the extent to which we see the people who come to us as being 'problems' or as people who have innate strengths and potential which can be utilised in tackling the difficulties which currently face them.

If we are honest, many people who are human services practitioners work with a 'deficit model' in their everyday practice. In other words, they make a basic set of assumptions about the people they work with which involves a degree of labelling. It goes something like this:

> We (the professional workers) are strong, capable, insightful, well-trained, resourceful, able to solve problems, and to be successful helpers. You (the service user/client), by contrast, are weak, unable to solve your problems, lacking insight, somewhat helpless, and therefore so fortunate to have us to work with you to give you the benefit of our skills and knowledge, so that some measure of improvement can be achieved in your mediocre lives.

This somewhat overstated caricature is likely to ring bells with human services practitioners precisely because so much professional training and practice (including assessment and intervention) is often implicitly based upon the model that 'the professional knows best'. Without doubt, such a model has its place, particularly when it comes to legal or medical expertise. But elsewhere in human services there are dangers in refusing to see that everyone has strengths and potential which can be encouraged and utilised in tackling difficulties and problems.

The first challenge therefore is precisely this: to what extent do we as human services practitioners have a world-view which recognises and celebrates the strengths which other people have, including those who come 'for help'? Is 'help' something which we as workers have in an abundant supply, and which in our bounty we then dispense to others less fortunate than ourselves; or is 'help' something which is intrinsically present within every person, but which may need someone else sometimes to release it within us?

The concept of a 'strengths perspective' is becoming increasingly important in human services. As Hodge (2003) notes:

> This framework posits clients' personal and environmental strengths as central to the helping process . . . without a reliable means for finding clients' strengths, practitioners tend to revert to practice models that are based upon the identification of problems and deficits. (p. 14)

Not for the first time the challenge comes to the human services worker, and raises questions about their own spirituality, their own world-view and what they do to give expression to it. The professional challenge for many human services workers is to take seriously the concept of 'partnership working' which now occupies a central place certainly within both the literature and practice. Perhaps the new challenge facing us, however, is not just to recognise a 'strengths perspective', but also to acknowledge that spirituality and the issues surrounding it are not the prerogative of the professional helpers, but are intrinsic to the human condition, whether or not they are openly acknowledged. One of the strengths to be explored for everyone, therefore, is the sense of what gives meaning and purpose to living, and how that can be enhanced and strengthened.

To take such partnership working seriously involves a recognition that for many people a spiritual or religious dimension to their lives is part of the 'strengths perspective' which human service workers need to take seriously, and not ignore. This is far more than the tokenistic tick sheet, closed question, approach which is dealt with in a split second, whatever the respondent's answer. It opens up the whole area of the ways in which a person's spiritual and religious perspective provides a major source of strength in times of difficulty. Apart from the nursing profession which has for a long time recognised the importance of this perspective at the individual level, other human services workers have been less sympathetic to this dimension. As Parsloe (1999) comments in connection with the requirement in the NHS and Community Care Act 1990 to carry out assessments:

> Many full assessments are carried out by local authority staff, often with assistance from medical and nursing staff as well. The assessment is meant to cover medical, social, financial and emotional needs. What is not included are spiritual needs . . . One might argue that social workers should be able to help their clients to talk about spiritual needs and help them find ways to meet them . . . but my experience of social workers is that . . . they seldom raise spiritual questions and I suspect that they sometimes make it difficult for clients to raise them. (p. 140)

Parsloe's concern can most likely be applied to a range of other human services workers, as can also her comments about training:

> Sadly their professional training plays into this rejection. I have noticed over the years that spiritual matters and religious concerns seem to have been taboo subjects on the university social work courses for which I have been responsible. No one talked about such matters. (p. 141)

This takes us back to some of the issues raised in the earlier discussions in this book, but the central point being stressed here from a practice perspective is the importance of recognising a 'strengths perspective' and the contribution which spirituality, and sometimes religion, can make to the people with whom we work. We need to recognise that we will be doing them a disservice if we neglect such issues. It is time that 'best practice' openly acknowledged the importance of these issues for all human services practitioners.

Alongside the 'strengths perspective' is another theme which deserves to be explored in the context of spirituality and religion, and that is the concept of 'resilience'. Resilience theory has a contribution to make in its own right to our understanding of children and young people. From the perspective of this book however there seem to be important insights into the contribution which religion and spirituality can make to people's lives, which may give a new direction to this important theoretical perspective.

New directions in resilience theory?

The contribution of resilience theory to our understanding of how children and young people cope with, and survive, experiences of great hurt and disadvantage, has already been noted. Indeed there is an increasing literature on this important subject and its implications to help us understand the phenomenon of overcoming stress or adversity (Rutter, 1999). This is a complex issue, where a number of factors influence the outcome. For example, Rutter (1999) found, in his exploration of resilence theory and its impact upon family therapy, that:

> The psychopathological effects of risk experiences are strongly moderated by how individuals cognitively and affectively process their experiences and how the resulting working model of relationships is integrated into their self-concept. (p. 139)

This seems to have close parallels with some of the issues being raised in this book. What Rutter seems to be suggesting, in effect, is that the child or young person is faced with the challenge of either incorporating their experience and understanding of adversity into their existing world-view, or alternatively to reshape their world-view in order to bring about a more comprehensive understanding. The more capable someone is of achieving this, the more resilient they are likely to be in the face of such adversity. Rutter argues that:

> For psychologically healthy adult development and relationships, people need to accept the . . . reality of the bad experiences they have had, and to find a way of incorporating the reality of these experiences into their own self-concept, but doing so in a way that builds on the positive while not denying the negative. (p. 135)

This has clear parallels with the discussions earlier in this book about the ways in which people's chosen world-views are, or are not, capable of incorporating new sets of experiences into a deeper understanding. Interestingly, it also has close parallels with Neimeyer's 'meaning reconstruction' theory which is making such an impact upon our understanding of the ways in which people reshape their world-views in the aftermath of significant loss (see Neimeyer and Anderson, 2002, for a useful introduction).

The contribution which resilience theory has made to our understanding of children's and young people's experiences of adversity seems capable of a wider application. Indeed, the whole concept of resilience seems to offer an important dimension to many of the issues being raised in this book.

Many people, for example, who belong to faith communities would want to claim that the world-view which they have adopted as a result of joining these groups provides an extra dimension which helps them both grapple with, and find intellectually and emotionally satisfying responses to, many of the big issues facing humanity. Those who believe, for example, that there is a further dimension to existence after death, often claim that this faith helps them put the experiences of grief and loss into a framework which helps them make more sense of it all. For such people, their religious faith is an important factor in developing their emotional resilience in the face of death, grief and loss. In a similar way, Muslims (and others) who believe that everything that happens to them has a purpose which ultimately must reflect the will and purpose of Allah, will want to argue that this too increases their emotional resilience and capacity to cope in the face of adversity. For those who belong to faith-based organisations, the love and care and support of others who belong to it provide a major boost to their emotional resilience in times of adversity.

This is not to suggest for one moment that people who do not belong to quite different organisations fail to receive similar levels of resilience-enhancing support from those who also belong to the same group. The point is similar in both cases: it is the acknowledgement that resilience is an important concept, and that a crucial question for everyone is to identify what enhances, and what reduces, this capacity within us. This capacity is especially important in times of difficulty, of course, and one further question to ask is the extent to which the organisations we belong to can make a contribution to this capacity for resilience. The importance of faith-based organisations is that part of their *raison d'être* is to focus explicitly on some of the very areas of living and dying which most greatly perplex people, and to offer a world-view which seeks to locate these painful and problematic experiences within a particular framework.

The same point may be made in connection with the wider issues of spirituality, which, as has been argued in this book, has strong connections with the issues of meaning and purpose, and our chosen world-views. However people may define spirituality, and whatever activities may flow from their chosen definition, one of the questions that can be legitimately asked is the extent to which that chosen world-view enhances their resilience in the face of adversity.

The links with the core values being discussed in this section – most especially the capacity to celebrate diversity – are clear. Does a person's, or for that matter an organisation's, world-view and value base enhance or diminish people's resilience? If, for example, a particular world-view sees black people, or women, or gay and lesbian people, or disabled people as essentially inferior to other members of the community, then that world-view may be seen as diminishing the resilience of black people, women, gay and lesbian people and disabled people *precisely because* of the limitations and restrictions it imposes upon those groups of people. By contrast, a world-view which celebrates diversity and welcomes the enrichment which everybody can make to the community as a whole can be seen to be enhancing resilience *precisely because* it values everyone's contribution.

In the sections which follow, this concept of resilience, and the extent to which religion and spirituality may enhance or diminish people's life-chances and opportunities, will be developed and applied. For the human services practitioner, this 'resilience test' may provide a crucial benchmark in assessing the contribution which various faith-based organisations may be making to an individual's well-being, and the extent to which it complements, or is at odds with, the value base of the agency which is seeking to help them.

The strengths perspective and the developments in resilience theory suggested above are closely interwoven, and from a practice perspective may be seen as near enough being the same thing when it comes to exploring issues with service users. There is, however, a third overlapping and interweaving theme which deserves exploration. This is the huge topic of power, to which briefly we now must turn.

Power

Without doubt one of the central themes for any human services practitioner to grapple with is the concept of power and how it is exercised both at an individual and also at organisational and structural levels.

As individual practitioners in the human services, there is an in-built 'power differential' between professional and service user to a greater or lesser extent. Those who work as detached street workers may be seen at one end of this spectrum because the young people with whom they work can decide whether or not to engage with them, and if they walk away there will be nothing the worker can do about it. At the other end of the spectrum are the probation officers and social workers whose power is legitimated by statute, and who can, if need be, play a key role in taking a person back to court for further punishment; in having a mentally disturbed person taken into psychiatric hospital against their will; or removing a child into care for safety and protection, with or without the parent's permission. Somewhere in the middle of the spectrum are people who work in hostels for homeless people, day centres or drug rehabilitation units, and who actively seek to engage people in their journey to recovery, but make no secret of the fact that, should core rules be broken, they will not hesitate in excluding that person from their centre.

As always, the extremes do not typify the bulk of a human service practitioner's work, but the boundaries always need to be clearly understood by all concerned. And boundaries locate where power lies in the relationship.

At the structural and organisational levels, issues of power are interwoven with professional accountability and also with the impact upon daily practice of the budgetary decisions of the department. No amount of partnership working with the individual or family will produce goods or services that the organisation cannot, or will not, pay for.

It may be tempting to conceptualise power as being solely in the hands of the recognisably powerful within government, industry, or various organisations, and then to lament the way in which it is wielded, as if power were something foreign to us. There is of course some undoubted truth in this certainly at the macro level of society, but to limit our understanding in such a way is to misunderstand the nature of power which pervades every aspect of human living. The person who sits in stony silence during an interview is exercising immense power, however disconcerting it may feel to the interviewer who is used to 'calling the shots'. One of the seminal theorists in this field, Foucault, saw power as a feature of all social relationships:

> What I am attentive to is the fact that every human relation is to some degree a power relation. We move in a world of perpetual strategic relations. (1988, p. 168, cited in Thompson, 2003, p. 52)

This has clear links with the discussion about strength perspectives in that Foucault's analysis encourages all of us, in whatever relationships or roles we are involved, to examine how we use the power we have, and in what ways it operates within our relationships, personal or professional. We each need to explore the impact of the power we exercise, and to assess whether it is being used in a positive and creative way, or in a negative, destructive manner. From a practice perspective, we can also earmark this issue as worthy of discussion with our service users, to share some dialogue with them about how they use power in their relationships, and the impact which it has upon others.

Furthermore, in terms of the issues which are central to this part of the book – anti-discriminatory, anti-oppressive, emancipatory practice; celebrating diversity, and the passion for justice at the heart of spirituality – the theme of power is of crucial importance. Power is not just about what we can *make* happen in a positive way; it is also about what we can *stop* happening. Power can be used to keep people from their just entitlements, as well as allowing equality of access and opportunity. As Thompson (2003) observes:

> Power is therefore a central feature of the struggle to promote equality. Indeed, the very term 'struggle' is a significant one, as it indicates that there are established structures and vested interests that are likely to stand in the way of progress. Promoting equality inevitably involves entering into conflict with the 'powers that be', the dominant social arrangements that help to maintain existing power relations. Consequently, we need to recognise that an understanding of the workings of power is an essential part of challenging inequality, discrimination and oppression. (p. 45)

Inevitably, this discussion needs to take for granted much of the substance of the theoretical debates about power which are explored and critiqued in the literature (see Thompson, 2003). For the purposes of this chapter, however, some attention will be given to a brief exploration into religious and spiritual perspectives on power, if only to illustrate the common concerns which exist between the secular theorists and theological perspectives.

The concept of power is a very familiar one to anyone who belongs to a faith community such as Christianity, Judaism or Islam. The world-views of these three monotheistic faiths are very similar in that their holy books – the Bible; the Torah and the Qur'an – proclaim that ultimate power belongs to the Supreme Being (God – Adonay – Allah) who not only brought all things into existence with creative power, but also continues to influence human affairs. For these faith communities all human power is in one sense derived from the divine source of power. The question then becomes a familiar one, about how power is used and exercised within human relationships for good or ill. Pre-dating Foucault by several centuries, these faith communities are very clear about the pervasive nature of power, and its capacity for either enriching or diminishing the human experience.

On the positive side, these faith communities all proclaim the life-enhancing benefits of faith whereby the power from the divine being can transform their lives, bring to them a sense of meaning and purpose and value, and provide a world-view that proclaims an ultimate triumph of good over evil. It also motivates many of them to strive for a more just, equal and tolerant society, and to work towards the eradication of poverty and starvation.

On the negative side, there are clear dimensions to their world-views which take evil very seriously as a powerful force in people's lives. In Christian theology, for example, St Paul talks about the 'principalities and powers of this dark age' (Ephesians Chap 6 v 12) with their negative impact upon human relationships, in terms which are not wildly different from our understanding of how oppression works to undermine the dignity and worth of many groups of people in contemporary society. This understanding of power mirrors Foucault's in that there is a clear understanding that the negative impact of 'mal-directed power' can operate just as forcefully within faith-based organisations as outside them. Discrimination and oppression can become major features of faith communities, as with any other organisation. There are also parallels here with the PCS analysis mentioned earlier in the discussion, which is a clear indication that faith communities often have an awareness of the complexity of the issues which face human communities, and the various levels at which discrimination and oppression operate. Furthermore, faith communities might want to argue for the same enrichment of PCS analysis as was proposed earlier, namely a PCSS framework for understanding these issues which includes an additional S for spiritual/religious dimensions. Within such a framework there would be a huge degree of commonality in the shared vision for, and struggle towards social justice and equality, inspired by the passion for justice which is at the heart of spirituality as defined in this book.

This chapter has sought to make some important links between what may be called the secular theoretical frameworks of anti-discriminatory, anti-oppressive emancipatory practice within the context of celebrating diversity, and what may be called the religious, spiritual and theological perspectives on these key issues. The key themes of a 'strengths perspective', resilience, and an understanding of power have found shared territory which, at very least, suggests that there may be more allies sharing a common struggle than many had previously suspected. From the practitioner's stand-point, however, it has raised the important awareness that religion and spirituality may highlight strengths, resilience and a thirst for social justice in people which mirrors the practitioner's own commitment to these core values. But this is not necessarily so. As we noted in Part One, religion in particular, but also spirituality can have a negative as well as a positive impact, and to the practice implications of this we need now to turn.

Chapter 11
Challenging Discrimination: Fostering Resilience

In Part One considerable space was devoted to an endeavour to present a balanced view about the positive and negative impact of religion and spirituality. Behind all these generalities, however, lies the truth that, for each person, the reality will be unique. How a person interprets and understands their spirituality will be unique to them, and may never be fully articulated, however sensitively the dialogue with a helping professional may be conducted. Indeed, one of the difficulties with this whole area of discourse about these aspects of human experience is the unavoidable lack of clarity when defining the terms being used, linked to the fact that for many people the language of religion and spirituality seems foreign to their world-view. Spirituality is seen by them as a marginal 'activity' which excites the interest of the fanatical few rather than something which illuminates and informs what it means for all of us to be human. And yet, from the perspective of the human services practitioner in whatever field or discipline, these are important issues to raise and grapple with, especially if it is accepted that resilience and a passion for justice are also part of this territory.

The definition of spirituality being offered in this book suggests that it is what we do to give expression to our chosen world-view. We are perhaps now in a better position to explore the practice perspectives of this definition, now that the context of anti-discriminatory, anti-oppressive and emancipatory practice have been explored as the value base for the helping professions. Furthermore, the suggestion that spirituality, and religion, can have a liberating, emancipatory role in people's lives which can foster resilience in dealing with the painful and sometimes tragic dimensions of human life, is one which human services practitioners need to take very seriously. Much of their work involves dealing with pain, change and loss in people's lives, and to have a framework which can offer a creative context for understanding and dealing with these issues is of huge significance. At times of crisis, people tend to ask the 'big' questions which raise issues about meaning and purpose in their lives, and how to make sense of events which challenge their previously held world-view. The challenge of this book for the helping professions is the extent to which they feel able to enter into some meaningful dialogue with people at this very point of inner discomfiture. In short, they can explore issues of spirituality, whether or not this word is actually used in their dialogue.

The definition being offered – spirituality is what we do to give expression to our chosen world-view – allows the helping professional to explore with people how they see the world, and what their chosen world-view looks like. Specifically, they can tease out the ways in which such world-views enable the people who hold them to offer a (perhaps moderately) satisfying attempt to make sense of what is happening to them and to others; the extent to which their chosen world-view provides strength and resilience to deal with adversity; and the framework it offers to them about how to regard and deal with other people. It is perhaps reasonable to suggest that for a world-view to be credible it must be able to a certain extent to satisfy all three of these criteria. In other words, for a world-view to be credible it must be able to provide for the person who holds it:

1. a satisfying framework to provide at least some answers to the 'big' questions about meaning and purpose in life;
2. an emotionally satisfying impact upon people which strengthens their capacity to deal with major losses and disasters, thereby increasing their resilience; and
3. a value base for how they behave towards others.

The third criterion is of particular interest for human services practitioners who often are dealing with the impact of people's behaviour upon other people. Probation officers, prison officers, social workers, and youth workers, for example, will often be seeking to change people's 'offending behaviour' (to use this well-established criminal justice 'mantra' for purposes of illustration). To have any chance of a successful change in such behaviour necessarily involves an exploration into the offender's world-view, and to review the implications and limitations of the chosen world-view for that particular person. The work of prison chaplains is illuminating at this point. Some of the 'success stories' which are recounted by chaplains frequently involve a major change of world-view on the part of the particular prisoners whose determination to 'go straight' stems from a particular 'conversion experience'; in other words, they take on a different world-view which then profoundly affects how they choose to behave.

Helping professionals, of course, are not allowed to proselytise or to persuade people to adopt a different world-view. This fear has been at the heart of much disquiet within the education and training of helping professionals. The dangers of exploiting vulnerable people at times of emotional distress are well known. Interestingly, however, the concern has traditionally always been directed at helping professionals who espouse a particular religious affiliation. Christian workers, for example, are always challenged on this very issue to make sure that their religious commitment does not compromise their professional values, and that they do not seek to 'convert' people through their professional intervention. This is absolutely right and fully accepted. What is fascinating in this context is that people who hold an atheist position, for example, or people who are fundamentally opposed to any valuing of spirituality, are not similarly challenged so explicitly. And yet perhaps they need just as much professional training in how to work sensitively with people of faith as committed members of faith-based organisations need in avoiding the dangers of proselytising. Both of these are examples of world-views which may or may not meet the three criteria outlined above as far as each individual is concerned. The important issue for the human services practitioner is the willingness, sensitivity and openness to explore these issues when appropriate with those who come to them for help.

One further example deserves mention, not least because it takes us into some complex issues for practice. Someone who belongs to the British National Party (BNP), for example, may feel that their chosen world-view satisfies all three criteria. From the perspective of the professional worker, however, there would be major concerns about a value base/world-view which not only treats people of colour disrespectfully, but also actively encourages violence against them. This flies in the face of the 'celebrating diversity' value base of the professional worker so fundamentally that it has to be challenged. The discriminatory and oppressive behaviour which such a world-view encourages is so alien not just to the professional value base, but also to the law of the land, that it has to be challenged. But the very act of challenging, with its demands that at very least people modify their behaviour or pay the consequences, has an element of proselytising to it, in that respect for individual dignity should be a non-negotiable tenet within contemporary UK society.

The issue of racial discrimination is but one of many examples that could be chosen. Two further examples involve the way in which women are regarded and treated, and how issues of human sexuality are dealt with, particularly within faith-based organisations. These are areas which often cause greatest concern for human services practitioners when working in a multi-faith, multicultural community.

The issues can be stark precisely because some faith-based organisations adopt principled positions on these issues which are based on doctrinal convictions derived from interpretations from their sacred writings. To those who have had no involvement with faith communities, this can be a confusing territory to explore, not least because there is a rich variety of interpretation within most, if not all, faith traditions. Some traditions within the Christian Church, for example, are strongly committed to inclusivity as a basic tenet of faith. They believe that the creative God whom they worship loves people equally and unreservedly, and that diversity is a God-given gift to the world which needs to reflected above all in the very communities which seek to give God their allegiance. Therefore everybody, irrespective of race, gender, or sexual orientation, needs to feel that they have a part to play within the Church, including leadership at all levels. If such a stance seems to be at odds with tradition and the sacred texts, the response is that the same creative God is not restricted by the past, but is ever leading people into newer and deeper understandings of what it means to be human and children of the creator. By contrast, other traditions within the Christian Church claim to be just as loyal to their creator God, and believe that they are under an obligation to respect, as they stand, the teachings of their sacred texts. If their interpretation of these texts means that women need to play a subservient role, and that only heterosexual love-making within a legally binding marriage is acceptable, then they see it as their clear duty to proclaim this, even if it does mean being out of step with contemporary values. Of far greater importance to them is an obedience to what they believe are eternal and unchanging truths which impact upon human behaviour.

These examples may be followed through in the other main monotheistic religions (Judaism and Islam), although there seems to be less clear evidence within Islam of what some may call the 'liberal' approach to human sexuality. However, in Patel's (1997) important book, one anonymous author comments powerfully, from an Asian female perspective, on the ways in which:

> Religious ethics are contaminated by a male political and economic agenda which turns women into dependants, and as a result, denies the equality, respect and control of their lives and the opportunity to contribute meaningfully to society. (p. 54)

The perplexity felt by helping professions is understandable. In terms of the framework being proposed in this book, it seems as if there is not just one Christian, Muslim, or Jewish world-view, but several almost competing world-views *within* each of these religions. And if the terms of reference are expanded to include the totality of religions, the confusion becomes absolute! And yet it is salutary to note that each of these faith-based organisations, whether they attract millions, thousands or only hundreds of adherents, are offering to their members a world-view which we must assume they find satisfying in terms of the three criteria offered earlier in this chapter. The challenge for the human services practitioner is not to feel that somehow they need to be 'expert' in their knowledge of these faith systems, but rather to feel confident and comfortable in exploring with people the ways in which their chosen world-view proves satisfying, and how it affects their behaviour especially towards others. So the emphasis is less on 'knowing about', and much more on the worker's willingness, ability and sensitivity to explore these issues with people whose choice of world-view may be quite alien to the worker's own.

The role of the helping professional may be summarised in the phrase used to head this chapter: *challenge* discrimination and *foster* resilience. The challenge to discrimination is, of course, familiar territory to some human services practitioners, especially social workers and probation officers. The value base discussed earlier provides a clear imperative for this. The particular sensitivity facing practitioners is when discrimination is practised in the name of a particular faith-based organisation which otherwise would be deemed to be playing a positive and constructive role within society. In some communities, for example, the role of women appears to be understood in very clear ways, and the expectations upon women to live within these boundaries is high. This can lead to some tensions between career and family expectations, and a clash between competing world-views, each of which genuinely believes that it is honouring and respecting the women in their community.

Here, of course, we enter the realms of very familiar debate about patriarchy, gender stereotyping, discrimination and oppression, which are important search-lights to be played upon the whole of society, not just upon specific faith-based organisations. The helping professions, however, often feel that the tightrope is more hazardous to balance upon when dealing with faith-based organisations. Should they collude with a system with which they fundamentally disagree, or does a respectful, professional approach demand that we start where the other person is to be found, even if that feels compromising to the worker? These are practice dilemmas which have no easy answer. These dilemmas are perhaps at their most acute (or perhaps they are most straightforward?) when issues of abuse are being explored. Is male or female circumcision, for example, ever justifiable, even if hallowed by religious tradition? How do we respond to issues of family discipline which to the worker might seem too severe, but which the family believe are part of their religious responsibility? Professional judgment is crucial here, as is a system of detailed recording, supervision and accountability, but ultimately anti-discriminatory practice provides the framework to tackle these complex issues.

When it comes to fostering resilience, we enter the wide arena of assessment. The requirements to include a religious/spiritual dimension to assessment have already been noted, even though this continues to be a much neglected area. Whether it be a comprehensive assessment on a older person, or assessing how to place a looked-after child; whether it be an assessment of potential foster parents or adopters, or engaging with someone facing a life-threatening illness; whether it be assessing disability issues or dealing with the complex network of loss – in all these issues and many more, resilience is an important factor to consider. As has already been argued, there is an important practice-focused link between a strengths perspective and resilience, both of which can be located within a spirituality framework.

It should not for one moment be assumed that a strengths perspective has a narrow focus for a practitioner. On the contrary, it is such a fundamental principle that it needs to be a core strand in the approach which all helping professions take. The very phrase 'helping professions', common though it is, runs the risk of suggesting that help is given uni-directionally, from the one who has to the one who has not; from the professional helper to the needy helpless service user/client. By contrast, a strengths perspective starts from the assumption – or from the world-view – that everyone has strengths, gifts, talents and abilities which can be used in their life-journey. There may well be occasions when major loss or trauma 'zaps' the energies, and reduces a person's capacity to cope temporarily. But the role of the human services practitioner is not to foster a sense of learned helplessness or dependence, but rather to be an enabling encourager who seeks to bring back to full strength the talents and capacity which is present in that person. The current buzz words of 'partnership working' and 'empowerment' are part of this process.

In the search for a particular person's strengths, it is important to take as holistic an approach as possible. It is here that the acknowledgement of spirituality and religion must be made. On some occasions it may well be that the previously tried and trusted world-view has been blown apart, or at least severely dented by the events which have brought the helping professional into their lives. In such cases it may well fall upon the practitioner to begin a dialogue and a gentle exploration which ultimately a better qualified spiritual or religious leader may need to take further. But the importance of giving a message to the person that it is all right to discuss such issues cannot be underestimated. There are occasions when people who belong to faith communities, for example, find it difficult to talk to their religious or spiritual leaders about the loss of faith brought about by some major event because they feel they are' letting the side down'. The core value of unconditional acceptance by the helping professional at this early stage may well play a major role in helping that person regain the strength they feel they have lost, and to undertake the at times costly journey of reconstructing a world-view which helps them make more sense of what has happened to them.

For others, however, it is their spiritual perspective or their religious faith which sustains them through difficult days and casts a rainbow of meaning around their apparently dark and hostile sky. This can become clear at times of great loss of bereavement; or in a more general sense they have a conviction that their future 'is in safe hands'. The Muslim conviction, shared to a greater or lesser degree by other faith systems, that everything that happens must, by definition, be according to the will of Allah, may appear mystifying to a non-believer, but to a devout Muslim it brings a sense of confidence and peace. This only comes, of course, with the acceptance of the Islamic world-view, but is an example of how resilience and a strengths perspective can be derived from a faith system. Human services practitioners need to acknowledge and respect such a view, even if it feels alien to their own world-view.

By contrast, a worker who belongs to a faith community would need to acknowledge and respect what we may call an 'atheistic spirituality', even if to them it seems to be a contradiction in terms. According to the definition of spirituality adopted for this book, however, such a position is perfectly tenable. Indeed, there are many who find strength and resilience *precisely from* the conviction that there is 'nothing more' to life or after life than what we can experience in our everyday living and loving. It is this sense of feeling more in control, rather than relying on some supreme being, which enhances their capacity for resilience. In such situations, best practice would be about acknowledging this and helping the person to celebrate their resilience, not about seeking to introduce a different world-view that the person had no wish, or need, to accept.

This chapter has explored two sides of a coin as far as practice issues are concerned. It has stressed the importance of a proper sense of discrimination which can distinguish between the good and bad effects of religion and spirituality, especially when it involves how people behave one towards the other. It has re-emphasised the importance of the value base of anti-discriminatory practice as a benchmark by which to evaluate the criteria for an 'effective' world-view. It has further emphasised the ways in which a strengths perspective is an important approach for human services practitioners to take in all their work, and that for many people spirituality in a general sense, and for some religion in particular, are important components for their own resilience which workers need to acknowledge and respect.

What this chapter, and indeed this book, has not done is to unpack and explore a range of detailed practice issues. This is perhaps the task for a companion volume to parallel in a UK context some of the work being done in the United States and Canada (see for example Scales *et al.*, 2002). Nevertheless, it is important to tackle at least one practice context to see some of the ways in which a spiritual perspective can enrich our understanding. It is to the area of mental health and spirituality, therefore, that we must now turn in the next chapter.

Chapter 12
Practice Snapshot: Religion, Spirituality and Mental Health

There is always a risk in a chapter such as this that those who feel an affinity with the topic area will press on and read it, whilst others for whom the subject holds less interest will simply skip over and ignore it. It is for this reason that the main thrust and approach of the book has been to deal with issues in a general way, rather than trying to unpack a series of perhaps 'single issue' topics. Mental health has been chosen, however, for several reasons. First, it is one of the comprehensive topics which cannot be limited to particular age groups with whom human service practitioners work. It is a pervasive and complex phenomenon that can affect us all. Second, it has attracted considerable interest among practitioners and academics who are fascinated by the interface between religion, spirituality and mental health in our multi-faith, multicultural society. Third, there has been national interest in these issues through the two-year partnership launched in November 2003 between the National Institute for Mental Health in England (NIMHE) and the Mental Health Foundation, which seeks 'to bring together and develop current thinking and practice in the area of spirituality and mental health' (NIMHE, 2003).

It is important to link in, at this point, the increasingly important concept of 'recovery' which has been highlighted by the Government. In its report *The Journey to Recovery* (DoH, 2001b) it comments that:

> Historically people with mental illness were often not expected to recover. For example, people with schizophrenia were generally perceived as having a poor outlook, having to live their life in a uniformly downward spiral of persistent symptoms.

> This perception has influenced the public view of people diagnosed as having mental illness, as being ultimately unable to take control of their lives and to recover . . . We need to create an optimistic, positive approach to all people who use mental health services. *The vast majority have real prospects of recovery* – if they are supported by appropriate services, driven by the right values and attitudes. (p. 24, emphasis added)

Within this context, the development of STR workers (DoH, 2003) – that is, people who are part of a mental health team who can provide **S**upport and **T**ime to those who use mental health services to promote and enable their **R**ecovery – may be seen to be a significant development in contributing to a 'whole person' approach to recovery, and to help identify and develop a person's resilience as part of that process. It will be precisely the spending of 'quality time' with people – if that is not too hackneyed a phrase – that the prospects of recovery will be enhanced. And in that process, the chances are high that each individual's chosen world-view will be uncovered, and the theme of spirituality as defined in this book, especially when linked to the concepts of a strengths perspective and resilience, will be encountered as part of their journey to recovery.

Finally, the Royal College of Psychiatry founded a special interest group for the study of spirituality and psychiatry in 1999, which attracted around 700 members in the first four years of its work. Professor Antony Sheehan, the Chief Executive of NIMHE and Group Head of Mental Health in the Department of Health expressed the issues thus:

> Spirituality is increasingly being identified by people with mental health needs *as a vital part of their mental well-being and recovery from ill-health;* and is coming to greater prominence in our multi-cultural society. (NIMHE, 2003, p. 1, emphasis added)

Sheehan's emphasis is important, not just because it mirrors the strengths perspective and resilience discussed in the last chapter, but because it represents an 'official' acknowledgement that spirituality is an important dimension to strength, wholeness and recovery. For too long a 'popular view' has prevailed which associated religion and spirituality with psychiatric and psychological symptoms: hallucinations; hearing voices; seeing visions; and generally manifesting a 'quirky' world-view that needed treatment so that 'normality' could return.

It may be helpful at this point to offer a brief review of some of the research findings about the positive impact of religion and spirituality upon mental health. We may perhaps take as read some of the more negative reactions people have experienced such as a burdensome, disabling sense of guilt and sin and lack of self-worth exacerbated by certain religious traditions; suicidal thoughts and actions sometimes on a community level (for example, the mass suicide at Waco, Texas, instigated by a self-styled religious leader); and the 'brain-washing' especially of young people by certain religious sects and communities.

By contrast, there is now an increasing body of research which is highlighting the significant part which spirituality and religion can play in a person's psychological well-being; or as Powell (2003, p. 1) aptly puts it: 'spirituality is good for your health'. He further observes that some research findings show that:

> The majority of people coping with mental disorder find themselves turning to their spiritual and religious beliefs to help them pull through. For instance, in one survey of psychiatric patients, over half went to religious services and prayed daily, and over 80 per cent felt that their spiritual beliefs had a positive impact on their illness, providing comfort and feeling of being cared for and not alone. (p. 1)

It is interesting also at this point to note that, in a World Health Organisation report (1998,) the following comment was made: 'Patients and physicians have begun to realise the value of elements such as faith, hope and compassion in the healing process'.

In his paper to a NIMHE conference on Spirituality and Mental Health (2003) Powell reviewed some of the evidence from research into the links between religion, spirituality and mental health which showed that:

- A 60 to 80 per cent correlation between religion or spirituality and better health was found in the areas of prevention, recovery and coping ability in a wide range of conditions, including high blood pressure, cerebro-vascular disease, heart disease, immune system dysfunction, improved coping with cancer; in living with pain and disability, and smoking prevention (Koenig *et al.* 2001).
- In the mental health field where stress is common to every kind of breakdown, the extraordinary effects of religion and spirituality are now just beginning to be recognised (Larson *et al.*, 2001). People with a spiritual or religious affiliation are up to 40 per cent less likely to get depressed that those who don't have such an affiliation. And when they do get depressed, they recover faster (McCullough and Larson, 1999).
- Suicide: adults over 50 who have never participated in religious activities are four times more likely to commit suicide than those who do (Nisbet *et al.*, 2000).
- Substance misuse: religious/spiritual commitment correlates with lower levels of substance abuse. The risk of alcohol dependency is 60 per cent greater when there is no religious affiliation (Miller, 1998).

These are but a few snapshots from Powell's survey, and although UK readers may cavil somewhat at the preponderance of USA-based research, the point is still well made. Religion and spirituality can no longer be disregarded: on the contrary they do seem to play a prominent role in recovery and well-being, and human services practitioners need to recognise this important dimension.

Not that many psychiatrists feel any better prepared to deal with these issues than other helping professionals, although the number who have joined the special interest group on spirituality is very encouraging. The situation over a decade ago looked somewhat different. Powell observes that:

> psychiatrists are not given any guidance about how to handle spiritual matters when they arise in the consultation and because they feel unskilled, the tendency is to gloss over such things.

> Yet it turns out that the majority of people coping with mental disorder do find themselves turning to their spiritual and religious belief to help them pull through . . . over 80 per cent felt that their spiritual belief had a positive impact on their illness, providing comfort and feeling of being cared for and not alone. Yet over a third of them did not feel able to discuss such things with their psychiatrists [Lindgren and

Courtney 1995]. Perhaps their intuition was spot on, for other research shows that whereas in the general population over 90 per cent have belief in God or a higher power, around only a third of psychiatrists and psychologists hold such beliefs. [Bergin and Jensen 1990] (The danger here is that psychiatrists may think that they represent the norm, when it is they who are atypical in this regard.) (p. 1)

As always it is important to put such research findings into context and not to assume that they can bear more weight than they merit. Findings in one culture or country do not easily transfer to another: maybe not at all, in some cases. What may have been true a decade ago may no longer be the case now. With these important caveats firmly in place, however, some valid points do emerge which are relevant to the present discussion.

First, there does seem to be a close parallel between the training issues in spirituality for psychiatrists and for other human services practitioners. It is not only social workers whose curricula often do not take these issues seriously; probation officers, youth workers and advice workers are likely to face a similar lack of serious exploration of these issues on their training courses.

Second, whatever hesitations some may have about research findings which suggest an extremely high predisposition towards spirituality and religion on the part of people who have mental health difficulties, it is sufficiently strong evidence to ensure that spirituality and religion are at least placed on the map and taken seriously in the UK context. If the evidence is affirming the positive contribution which religion and spirituality can make towards positive mental health generally, and to increasing the resilience and strength perspectives for people recovering from mental ill-health, then again the issues need to be placed firmly on the training and education agenda.

Third, people who experience mental health difficulties often find their world-view is challenged. People, and frames of reference, which previously had seemed reliable can begin to appear to be less trustworthy. While it is perfectly true that a return to robust health can be accompanied by a return of confidence in the previous world-view, for others the experience of mental ill-health can lead to a reshaping of a world-view which remains intact after recovery has been achieved. The emphasis being made in this book upon the importance of a world-view, and what we do to give expression to it, becomes particularly significant, therefore, in issues to do with mental health.

Finally, it is important to pay heed to Powell's observation, no matter in what area of human services we work, about those many patients who felt unable to raise with their psychiatrist anything to do with religion and spirituality, even though these were significant features in their own journey to recovery. They obviously felt that this was a 'no go' area as far as therapy and treatment were concerned. This raises important issues for anyone working in the helping professions. To what extent do we consciously or subconsciously give off messages to those with whom we work that there are certain 'no go' areas into which we do not wish them to trespass? That we all have such areas is beyond doubt, and for many practitioners the territory of religion and spirituality is one into which any journeying, however tentative, seems to be fraught with uncertainty, even anxiety *on the part of the worker.* This is the key point: it is the *worker's* world-view which is somehow being challenged, and until we can reach the point where we can show the respect and dignity to those who wish, and at times really need, to talk about such issues with us, then we shall never reach that ultimate goal of 'best practice' which all of our service users so deeply deserve. The implication of this, however, is that there is an obligation upon all human services practitioners to have a sufficiently mature level of self-awareness to be comfortable enough with these issues to share that journey with those whom they are seeking to help, and not to allow any misgivings, or their own particular and different world-view, to put up the 'no entry' barriers to those for whom such issues are an important feature of the landscape.

Part Four: Guide to Further Learning

This book can only be seen as an introduction to the key themes which have been explored. It will have served its purpose well if it quickens the interest in those who read it, and encourages them on a journey to discover more about these key issues.

The spirit in which this book has been written however suggests that the starting point for further learning is not to hare round to the library, or into a Google search, for key terms in order to increase the volume of information at our command. We have already noted that this would be a task of gigantic proportions, doomed to ultimate disappointment. Instead it is suggested that the best place to start is with ourselves, and our own personal journey.

In Ancient Greece, much store was laid upon the oracle at Delphi where pilgrims would go to receive insight and wisdom. They were greeted with the inscription 'know thyself', and this perhaps is the best place for any of us to begin. Spirituality has been defined in this book in terms with which many, perhaps all practitioners can identify. We all have a chosen world-view, and how we live our lives, in large ways or small, is in response to that. So a major starting point is this personal reflection about who we are, and what are the priorities we place centre stage in our own lives.

The big questions which were identified earlier in this book are big questions for us too.

- How do we cope in the face of adversity?
- Are we resilient? In what ways does our world-view enhance that resilience? Or, if we are honest, do we find our world-view is a bit ragged round the edges at times and does not really 'pass muster'?
- What 'colours of meaning' do we throw round our lives to make some sense at least of what happens to us and those around us?
- What meaning do we give to our mortality?
- What does it mean to be human and to have the capacity to change?

How each of us deals with these, and other equally profound questions, is very much a matter of personal choice, of course. Some will find the framework of a faith community's world-view satisfying; others will look elsewhere. But it is important that somehow we each of us develop that level of self-awareness, so that we feel comfortable about the journey which it entails. For these are the journeys which many of the service users we encounter are also making, however vague the details may be articulated. And if we cannot share that journey to some extent at least, we are not providing a best-practice framework for our professional encounters with them.

It would be unwise to underestimate the importance of human contact in this journey. There is in some ways no substitute for meeting with people who hold particular world-views to explore with them their significance and the impact their views have upon their behaviour. Whether or not you belong to a faith community, it can be helpful to arrange to meet and discuss issues with people who see the world from a different perspective. Study sessions or seminars can be held with invited guests to explore together some issues of common concern, for it is in the experience of the shared journey that the most effective learning can take place. It is also in the experience of a shared vulnerability – for who among us has all the answers! – that a deeper enrichment can be shared. The shared concern to discover what various people do 'to give expression to their chosen world-view' is in itself an aspect of spirituality in which we all can participate, particularly if we have a commitment to reflective practice. Such issues can even make their way onto supervision agendas at individual and team level!

Within this spirit of honest enquiry, however, where we recognise that the journey can at times be as much ours as of those who we seek to help, there is an increasing range of material to help and encourage us on this journey.

Each of the books in the bibliography can offer some useful insights into the themes explored in this book, and the reading lists which each of these contains can send people on a further journey of discovery.

There is an increasing number of useful websites available. These include:

www.thegoodwebguide.co.uk – useful as a navigation tool around world religions

www.beliefnet.com – this provides a one-step gateway to gain the views of various religions on current issues, as well as providing information about core beliefs (NB You need to register on this site, but registration is free).

http://about.com/religion – has sections on various issues of topical interest

There are websites produced by particular churches which also have a wider appeal and interest. The Church of England for example offers two:

www.anglicansonline.org

www.anglicancommunion.org

Similarly, the Roman Catholic Church offers a variety of sites. The following two are worth looking at because of their emphasis upon social justice issues, and against extremism:

www.catholic-pages.com – a large complex site with a useful section on issues to do with social justice.

www.cafod.org.uk – obviously focusing on the work of CAFOD (the Catholic Agency for Overseas Development), this site illustrates very vividly 'faith in action' and the social justice aspect of spirituality.

Two sites from a Jewish perspective are
http://aish.com and www.chiefrabbi.org, the latter being particularly interesting
to see how a religious leader tackles issues of extremism.

Islam

www.islam.org – this provides a range of Muslim perspectives, while
www.islamicity.com takes a clear stand against extremism.

Hinduism

www.hindu.org – covers a wide range of issues and approaches to various
religious perspectives in a non-judgemental and very informative way.

Paganism

www.druidnetwork.org – provides fascinating insights into the growing appeal of
this fast-growing faith-based community.

In the fast-moving world of Internet information, it is always best to explore
issues of interest through a major search engine and discover just how much
there is out there on these fascinating themes. It is worth noting, however, that it
is not always easy to judge the 'bona fides' of websites which claim to represent
various religious and/or spiritual perspectives. Here, as elsewhere on the Internet,
a degree of caution is necessary in order to distinguish between official sites
which seek to reflect the beliefs and activities of a particular faith-based
organisation, and other less official and more individualistic sites which seek to
push a particular point of view.

Epilogue

This book does not have a conclusion, or a neat and tidy ending. With such issues as the ones with which we have been grappling, a conclusion might suggest that the journey has reached a far more clearly defined destination than it has. Instead, an epilogue is offered, not just because it mirrors the opening prologue and has a slightly religious or spiritual ring to it, but because it suggests the appropriateness of some closing comments as one pauses to take breath on the next stage of the journey.

Some huge themes have been attempted, in exploring and trying to bring some definition to what are admitted complex, even contentious issues. One principal aim however has been to argue that religion and spirituality are not the marginal activities and world-views which many would claim them to be, and which cause some human services practitioners to consign them to their trash can of irrelevance. On the contrary, there are many influences now at work which mean that these issues need to be given the serious attention which they deserve.

This has meant inevitably that the perplexing question of definition has had to be tackled. The literature has already offered a range of interesting and helpful definitions which have been reviewed in this book, and which many have found to be helpful and illuminating. In offering (yet) another definition – that spirituality is what we do to give expression to our chosen world-view – it has not been the intention to add to confusion, but rather to offer an approach which can be helpful to the human services practitioner in tackling the range of issues which come their way. This 'practice-orientated' definition gives to practitioners a 'handle' to develop ways of tackling these complex themes, without giving the impression that service users (or even workers) have to learn a completely new language before we can begin to communicate in this area. It offers a genuinely interested approach to someone by enquiring into:

- what 'turns that person on' and makes their life worthwhile;
- what gives them a sense of meaning and purpose;
- why do they do '*this* set of things' rather than '*that* set of things' and behave in *this* way rather than *that* way;
- what sustains them in times of crisis and difficulty; and
- how far is an experience of resilience being developed through their chosen world-view.

All these topics have been seen in the preceding discussions to be in the territory of both spirituality and religion, to a greater or lesser degree. In this sense at least, people may find themselves using slightly different language to describe already familiar experiences and approaches to life. The 'penny may suddenly drop' for some, as they encounter the definition being offered in this book: 'so *that* is what is meant! I hadn't realised before!'.

This definition also seeks to overcome what is so often seen as the religion-spirituality 'divide'. Often the discussions tend to enter the '1066 and all that' territory, with 'religion being a bad thing' and 'spirituality being a good thing'. Tempting though this may be to some, it is a false divide. For one thing it ignores the potential for positive and negative influences to be at work in both phenomena. To suggest that one can be all good and the other all bad is naïve in the extreme. The definition in this book seeks, by contrast, to provide for the practitioner a template which can be used to evaluate the impact and influence which a person's world-view has upon their attitudes, values and behaviour. To what extent does a person's chosen world-view enrich their understanding of the world and the people with whom they live and work? How far does it spur them on to challenge discrimination and oppression, or to what extent does it make them adopt discriminatory behaviour towards others? To what extent does their world-view encourage them to celebrate diversity, or to become narrowly partisan and bigoted? In other words, this definition enables the practitioner to explore the impact of a person's religion and spirituality in very practical and applied ways.

It has further implications for the worker. This definition moves beyond the approach which is often taken by educators and trainers who see the issue being best tackled by giving as much information about various faith-based communities, their customs, beliefs and practices, so that the helping professionals, in whatever sphere they choose to practise, will be well informed. Without doubt, in our multicultural, multi-faith society, all human services practitioners need to have developed a degree of multicultural, multi-faith awareness in order to offer a sensitive service to any who come to them. But any hope of becoming fully informed is a myth of Sisyphean proportions: just as we think we have got the full picture, the stone of our ignorance begins to roll back onto us, and the burden becomes unbearable as we realise we will never know enough. By contrast, the definition offered in this book both recognises and celebrates that it is the *service user* who is the expert, and encourages the worker to explore with them what are the implications in *their* lives of their chosen world-view, whether or not it has a specifically faith-based dimension.

This definition also makes it clear that the worker/service user divide is by no means as clear-cut as many think. Of course, there are professional boundaries between worker and service user which must be observed, and best practice demands that an appropriate, well-thought through and partnership-based approach to the issues being raised is developed and implemented. But eventually the worker will walk away, and the service user will be left, hopefully better able to face the future more creatively than before, but no longer having a professional worker 'in tow'. All this is important and is rightly stressed. But, unlike some areas of worker/service user contact, where the worker may well feel that they have nothing in common with the person with whom they are working, and that they are as different as 'chalk and cheese', when it comes to the definition offered in this book there is a commonality between them which some might find disconcerting. It is not just service users who choose a world-view: everyone does, implicitly or explicitly. Worker and service user alike have a chosen world-view which has an impact upon their values, their behaviour and the way in which they treat other people. Everyone has gone through a similar process of deciding what the world is like and how we are to respond to it, even if the responses we come up with radically differ. From the practice perspective, therefore, which is central to this book, this definition allows everyone to recognise that this is common territory in being human. The worker must not, of course, seek to 'convert' a service user to the worker's own chosen world-view, whether that be faith based or not, but the common shared experience of living as a consequence of a chosen world-view is something which can enrich a practitioner's work.

The definition, however, is not self-standing from a practice perspective. It has been stated clearly that there is a professional value base which underpins it, and which in some ways provides an interpretative template to help a practitioner engage with the person coming to them for help, and to evaluate their behaviour. The core value base of anti-discriminatory practice, with its interweaving themes of anti-oppressive and emancipatory practice, celebrating diversity, and (as we have argued in this book), the added enrichment of a strengths perspective and a development of resilience in the face of adversity, is an impressive yet fundamental foundation upon which all human services practice should be built. Important though spirituality and religion are in many people's lives, and even if in some respects their adherents may sometimes make claims which are 'beyond this world', when it comes to human services practice, the value base of anti-discriminatory practice in all its richness must remain intact.

From a theoretical perspective the PCS analysis so often applied to anti-discriminatory practice to highlight its complexity and richness, may be seen to be further developed by the themes being explored in this book. The existing themes of this analysis are not to be regarded as being watertight compartments. The 'personal', 'cultural' and 'structural' all to some extent interweave in their complexity and impact. The issues raised in this book concerning spirituality (into which for these theoretical purposes religion is being subsumed) bring an added dimension. It has been argued, therefore, that this theoretical framework may be creatively expanded into a PCSS model, where the dimension of the spiritual may be added to the other dimensions. As with the other three, there is no suggestion of it being a watertight compartment on its own, but rather a dimension which must not be ignored if full justice is to be done to a person's experience and chosen world-view. In this respect it can be seen, therefore, as the complete benchmark for best practice to which all human services practitioners should aspire.

References

Bauman, Z. (1997) *Post Modernity and its Discontents*, Oxford, Polity Press.

Beck, V. (1992) *Risk Society: Towards a New Modernity*. London, Sage.

Bergin, A. and Jensen, J. (1990) 'Religiosity of Psychotherapists: A National Survey', *Psychotherapy* 27: pp. 3–7.

Biestek, F. (1957) *The Casework Relationship*, Chicago, Chicago University Press.

Bowpitt, G. (1998) 'Evangelical Christianity, Secular Humanism, and the Genesis of British Social Work', *British Journal of Social Work* 28: pp. 675–693.

Bradford, J. (1995) *Caring for the Whole Child: A Holistic Approach to Spirituality*, London, The Children's Society.

Brandon, D. (2000) *Tao of Survival: Spirituality in Social Care and Counselling*, Birmingham, Venture Press.

Canda, E. and Furman, L. (1999) *Spiritual Diversity in Social Work Practice: The Heart of Helping*, New York, The Free Press.

Canda, E. and Smith, E. (eds) (2003) *Transpersonal Perspectives on Spirituality in Social Work*, New York, The Howarth Press.

Channer, Y. (1998) 'Understanding and Managing Conflict in the Learning Process: Christians Coming Out', in Cree and McCaulay (1998).

Cnaan, R. (1999) *The Newer Deal: Social Work and Religion in Partnership*, New York, Columbia University Press.

Cree, V. and McCaulay, C. (eds) (1998) *Transfer of Learning in Professional and Vocational Education*, London, Routledge.

Crompton, M. (1998) *Children, Spirituality, Religion and Social Work*, Aldershot, Ashgate.

Dalrymple, J. and Burke, B. (1995) *Anti-Oppressive Practice*, Open University Press.

Daniel, B., Wassell, S. and Gilligan, R. (1999) 'It's Just Common Sense Isn't It? Exploring Ways of Putting the Theory of Resilience into Action', *Journal of Adoption and Fostering* 23: (3), pp. 6–15.

Department of Health (1998) *Adoption: Achieving the right balance*. Local Authority circular LAC (98) 20.

Department of Health, Department for Education and Employment and the Home Office (2000) *Framework for the Assessment of Children in Need and their Families*, London, The Stationery Office.

Department of Health (2001a) *The Children Act Now: Messages from Research. Studies in Evaluating the Children Act 1989*, London, The Stationery Office.

Department of Health (2001b) *The Journey to Recovery: – The Government's Vision for Mental Health Care*, London, Department of Health.

Department of Health (2003) *Mental Health Policy Implementation Guide: Support, Time and Recovery (STR) Workers*, London, Department of Health.

Derezotes, D. (2001) Transpersonal Social Work with Couples: A compatibility-intimacy model. in Canda, E. and Smith, D. New York, The Howarth Press.

Doka, K. (2002) 'How Could God? Loss and the Spiritual Assumptive World', in Kauffman (2002).

Doka, K. and Morgan, J.D. (eds) (1993) *Death and Spirituality*, Amityville, NY, Baywood.

DiBlasio, F.A. (1993) 'The Role of Social Workers' Religious Beliefs in Helping Family Members Forgive', *Families in Society*, 74: (3), pp. 167–170.

Durkheim E. (1912) *The Elementary Forms of the Religious Life*, London, George, Allen & Unwin.

Ellis, M. (2000) *Revolutionary Forgiveness: Essays on Judaism, Christianity and the Future of Religious Life*, Waco, Texas, Baylor University Press.

Eliade, M. (1959) *The Sacred and the Profane: The Nature of Religion*, New York, Harcourt, Brace and World.

Eliot, T.S. (1944) *Four Quartets*, London, Faber and Faber.

Etzioni, A. (1995) *The Spirit of Community: Rights, Responsibilities and the Communitarian Agenda*, London, Fontana.

Farnell, R., Furbey R., Shams, al Haqq, Hills, S., Macey, M. and Smith, G. (2003) *'Faith' in Urban Regeneration? Engaging Faith Communities in Urban Regeneration*, Joseph Rowntree Foundation, The Policy Press.

Forgiveness Project (1993) Exhibition: 'The F Word : Images of Forgiveness' Held 23–28/12/03 at www.the.gallery@oxo. London, www.theforgiveness project.com/news/

Foucault, M. (1988) *Politics, Philosophy, Culture: Interviews and Other Writings 1977–1984*, New York, Routledge.

Franz, T. *et al.* (2001) 'Positive Outcomes of Losing a Loved One', in Neimeyer (2001).

Feuerbach, L. (1941) *The Essence of Christianity*, reissued (1957) New York, Harper Row. First published in 1841.

Furman, L., Benson, P., Grimwood, C. and Canda, E. (2004) 'Religion and Spirituality in the Social Services', *British Journal of Social Work*, 34: pp. 767–791.

Gamston, P. (2002) *A Study of the Contemporary Relationship Between Evangelical Christianity and Social Work in Terms of Stated Aims and Actual Practice at Organisational Levels*, Unpublished Masters Thesis, University of Reading.

Garvin, C. (ed.) (1998) Special Issue: Forgiveness. Reflections. *Narratives of Professional Helping* 4: (4) pp. 1–72.

Gibran, K. (1980) *The Prophet*, London, Pan Books (originally published 1926).

Giddens, A. (1991) *Modernity and Self-Identity: Self and Society in the Late Modern Age*, Cambridge, Polity Press.

Giddens, A. (2001) *Sociology*, 4th edn, Cambridge, Polity Press.

Gilbert, P. (2003) *The Value of Everything: Social Work and its Importance in the Field of Mental Health*, Lyme Regis, Russell House Publishing.

Gilligan, R. (1997) 'Beyond Permanence? The Importance of Resilience in Child Placement Practice and Planning', *Journal of Adoption and Fostering* 21: pp. 12–20.

Gordon, H. (2000) 'Guilt: Why is it Such a Burden?', *Bishop John Robinson Fellowship Newsletter* 9: pp. 4–6.

Habermas, J. (1973) *Legitimation Crisis*, London, Heinemann.

Haider, Ali J. (2002) *Child Abuse and Islam*, Paper presented to the World Association of Muslim Mental Health.

Halman, L. and Pettersson, T. (2001) 'Religion and Social Capital in Contemporary Europe: Results from the 1999/2000 European Values Study', *Research in the Social Scientific Study of Religion*, 12: pp. 66–93.

Haralambos, M., Holborn, M. and Heald, R. (2000) *Sociology: Themes and Perspectives*, 5th edn, London, HarperCollins.

Harris, M., Halfpenny, P. and Rochester, C. (2003) 'A Social Policy Role for Faith-Based Organisations? Lessons from the UK Jewish Voluntary Sector', *Journal of Social Policy* 32: (1), pp. 93–112.

Henery, N. (2003) 'The Reality of Visions : Contemporary Theories of Spirituality in Social Work', *British Journal of Social Work* 33: (8), pp. 1105–1113.

Hodge, D. (2003) *Spiritual Assessment: Handbook for Helping Professionals*, Botsford, CT.

Hunt, S. (2002) *Religion in Western Society*, Basingstoke, Palgrave Macmillan.

Hutchison, E. (2003) *Dimensions of Human Behavior: Person and Environment*, 2nd edn, London, Sage.

James, W. (1982) *The Varieties of Religious Experience*, New York, Penguin Books.

Jewell, A. (ed.) (1999) *Spirituality and Ageing*, London, Jessica Kingsley.

Kauffman, J. (ed.) (2002) *A Theory of Traumatic Loss*, New York and Hove, Brunner Routledge.

Koenig, H., McCullough, M. and Larson, D. (2001) *Handbook of Religion and Health*, Oxford, Oxford University Press.

Kubler-Ross, E. (1969) *On Death and Dying*, New York, Macmillan.

Lesser, W.A. and Vogt, E. (1972) *Reader in Comparative Religion: An Anthropological Approach*, 3rd edn, New York, Harper and Row.

Lindgren, K. and Coursey, R. (1995) 'Spirituality and Serious Mental Illness: A Two Part Study', *Psychosocial Rehabilitation Journal* 18: (3), pp. 93–111.

Lloyd, M. (1996) 'Philosophy and Religion in the Face of Death and Bereavement', *Journal of Religion and Health* 35: (4).

Lloyd, M. (1997) 'Dying and Bereavement, Spirituality and Social Work in a Market Economy of Welfare', *British Journal of Social Work* 27: (2), pp. 175–90.

Mannheim, K. (1936) *Ideology and Utopia: An Introduction to the Sociology of Knowledge*, New York, Harcourt, Brace and World.

Maslow, A. (1962) *Toward a Psychology of Being*, New York, Von Nostrand.

McCullough, M. and Larson, D. (1999) 'Religion and Depression: A Review of the Literature', *Twin Research* 2: pp. 126–136.

Morgan, J.D. (1993) 'The Existential Quest for Meaning', in Doka and Morgan (1993).

Miller, W. (1998) 'Researching the Spiritual Dimension of Alcohol and Other Drug Problems', *Addiction* 93: (7), pp. 979–990.

Moss, B. (2002) 'Spirituality: A Personal Perspective', in Thompson (2002b).

Neimeyer, R. (ed.) (2001) *Meaning Reconstruction and the Experience of Loss*, Washington, DC, American Psychological Association.

Neimeyer, R. and Anderson, A. (2002) 'Meaning Reconstruction Theory', in Thompson (2002a).

Nesbitt, P. (ed.) (2001) *Religion and Social Policy*, Walnut Creek, CA and Oxford, AltaMira Press.

Nisbet, P., Duberstein, P., Yeates, C. and Seidlitz, L. (2000) 'The Effect of Participation in Religious Activities on Suicide Versus Natural Death in Adults 50 and Older', *Journal of Nervous and Mental Disorder* 188: (8), pp. 543–546.

National Institute for Mental Health in England (NIMHE) (2003) *Inspiring Hope: Recognising the Importance of Spirituality in a Whole Person Approach to Mental Health*, Leeds, NIMHE.

Nurnberg, A. (1995) *Know your Rights*, London, UNICEF.

Parsloe, P. (1999) 'Some Spiritual and Ethical Issues in Community Care for Frail Elderly People: A Social Work View', in Jewell (1999).

Patel, N., Naik, D. and Humphries, B. (1998) *Visions of Reality: Religion and Ethnicity in Social Work*, London, Central Council for Education and Training in Social Work.

Phillipson, J. (1992) *Practising Equality: Women, Men and Social Work*, London, CCETSW.

Powell, A. (2003) *Psychiatry and Spirituality: The Forgotten Dimension*, Brighton, Pavilion/NIMHE.

Quiller Couch, A. (1923) *Armistice Day Anniversary Sermon*, Cambridge, November.

Rutter, M. (1999) 'Resilience Concepts and Findings: Implications for Family Therapy', *Journal of Family Therapy* 21: pp. 119–144.

Rutter, M. (2000) 'Resilience Re-considered: Conceptual Considerations, Empirical Findings and Policy Implications', in Shankoff and Meisels (2000).

Robertson, R. (1970) *The Sociological Interpretation of Religion*, Oxford, Blackwell.

Scales, T.L. *et al.* (eds) (2002) *Spirituality and Religion in Social Work Practice*, Alexandria, VA., Council on Social Work Education.

Shankoff, J.P. and Meisels, S.J. (eds) (2000) *Handbook of Early Childhood Interventions*, Cambridge, Cambridge University Press.

Smith, G. (2001) *Faith Makes Communities Work: A Report on Faith-based Community Development*, sponsored by the Shaftesbury Society and the Department of the Environment, Transport and the Regions. London, DETR

Stroebe, M. and Schut, H. (1999) 'The Dual Process Model of Coping with Bereavement: Rationale and Description', *Death Studies* 23: (3).

Swinton, J. (2001) *Spirituality and Mental Health Care: Rediscovering a 'Forgotten' Dimension*, London, Jessica Kingsley Publishers.

Tanyi, R. (2002) 'Towards Clarification of the Meaning of Spirituality', *Journal of Advanced Nursing* 39: (5), pp. 500–509.

Thakur, S. (1996) *Religion and Social Justice*, Basingstoke, Macmillan – now Palgrave Macmillan.

Thompson, N. (1991) *Crisis Intervention Revisited*, Birmingham, Pepar.

Thompson, N. (2001) *Anti-discriminatory Practice*, 3rd edn, Basingstoke, Palgrave Macmillan.

Thompson, N. (ed.) (2002a) *Loss and Grief: A Guide for Human Services Practitioners*, Basingstoke, Palgrave Macmillan.

Thompson, N. (2002b) 'Developing Anti-discriminatory Practice', in Tomlinson and Trew (2002).

Thompson, N. (2003) *Promoting Equality: Challenging Discrimination and Oppression*, 2nd edn, Basingstoke, Palgrave Macmillan.

Tomlinson, D. and Trew, W. (2002) *Equalising Opportunities: Minimising Oppression*, London, Routledge.

Weller, P. (1997) *Religions in the UK: A Multi-faith Directory*, Derby, University of Derby.

Weller, P. (2004) 'Identity, Politics and the Future(s) of Religion in the UK: The Case of the Religious Questions in the 2001 Decennial Census', *Journal of Contemporary Religion* 19: (1), pp. 3–21.

Williams, B. cited in Pettit, P. and Schwieso, J. (eds) (1995) *Aspects of the History of British Social Work*, Thesis: Faculty of Education and Community Studies, University of Reading. References cited by Gamston, P. (2002).

Wood, R. (1997) 'Social Capital and Political Culture: God Meets Politics in the Inner City', *American Behavioural Scientist*, 40: (5), March/April. pp. 595–605.

Worden, W.J. (1991) *Grief Consulting and Grief Therapy: A Handbook for the Mental Health Practitioner*, London, Routledge.

World Health Organisation (1998) Spirituality, Religiousness and Personal Beliefs: Report on WHO consultation. Geneva, WHO.

Index